PICKLING AND FERMENTING

Cookbook For Preppers

DISCOVER ESSENTIAL PRESERVING TECHNIQUE | A COMPLETE BEGINNER'S GUIDE WITH OVER 100 EASY AND TASTY RECIPES FOR A YEAR-ROUND SELF-SUFFICIENT PANTRY

Sophie Magnant

TABLE OF CONTENTS

INTRODUCTION 10

CHAPTER 1

Introduction to Pickling and Fermenting as Food
Preservation 11
History and Importance of Food Preservation Methods 12
Difference between Pickling and Fermentation 12
Nurturing Gut Health through Fermented Foods 12

CHAPTER 2

Pickling 14
Basic Principles of Pickling 14
How Does Pickling Work? 14
Different Pickling Methods 15
Other Pickled Products.. 15

CHAPTER 3

Preparation for Pickling 17
Selection of Products.. 17
Selection of Ingredients... 17
Equipment and Tools Required for Pickling 19

CHAPTER 4

Safe Storage Methods and Pickling Process....................20
Proper Pickling Techniques 20
Storing Pickled Foods Safely 20
Acidity Levels in Food Preservation 20
Guide to Pickle Processing Methods 21
Guidelines for Low-Temperature Pasteurization.............................. 21
Jar and Lid Preparation for Canning 21
Canning Packing Techniques... 22
Filling Jar 23
Control Headspace 23
Canning Process for Pickles 23
Cooling and Sealing Process for Canned Jars................................. 23

Guidelines for Storing Home-Canned Foods.................................... 24
Step-by-Step Guide to Water Bath Canning.................................... 25
Detailed Steps for the Pressure Canner Process 26

CHAPTER 5

Fermentation 28
The Art of Fermentation.. 28
Benefits of Fermented Foods 29
Basic Principles of Fermentation 30
Various Types of Fermentation 30
Spontaneous Fermentation vs. Starter Cultures.......................... 31
Lactic Fermentation 31

CHAPTER 6

Starting Your Fermentation Project.................................. 32
Essential Fermentation Tools and Equipment 32
Selecting Your Fermentation Vessel 33
Weighting and Covering.. 33
Quality Control Tools.. 34
Safety and Basic Techniques 34
Fermentation Time and Temperature Control.............................. 34
Checking Progress.. 34
Storing Fermented Vegetables 34
Important Tips... 35
Self-Brining and Added-Brine Approaches 35
Choosing Your Method.. 36
Preparing Vegetables for Fermentation.. 36

CHAPTER 7

Monitoring, Storage, and Troubleshooting..................... 37
Monitoring Temperature and Time 37
Simplified Guide to Monitoring pH: 38

CHAPTER 8

Signs Your Fermented Vegetables Are Ready.................. 40
Understanding When Fermented Vegetables Are Ready for
Consumption.. 40
Initial Stages of Fermentation: A Delicate Balance 40
Signs Your Fermented Vegetables Are Ready 40
Tips for Fermentation Newbies... 41
Recognize and Prevent Molds and Kahm Yeasts 41
Quick Guide on Mold and Kahm Yeast in Fermented Foods.............. 42

CHAPTER 9

Pickling Recipes **43**

Vegetables 44

1. Dilled Pickled Beans 44
2. Green Tomato Dill Pickles 44
3. Beetroot Pickles 45
4. Carrot Pickles 46
5. Banana Pepper Rings Pickles 46
6. Dilled Okra Pickles 47
7. Marinated Mushrooms 47
8. Bread and Butter Zucchini Pickles 48
9. Horseradish Pickles Sauce 49
10. Hot Peppers Pickles 50
11. Asparagus Pickles 50
12. Brussels Sprouts Pickles with Turmeric 51
13. Cauliflower Pickles with Turmeric and Ginger 52
14. Sweet Peppers Pickles 53
15. Sweet Green Cherry Tomato Pickles 54

Fresh-pack or Quick-process Recipes 55

16. Pickled Mustard Cucumber 55
17. Quick Dill Pickles 55
18. Classic Bread and Butter Pickles 56
19. Quick Sweet Pickled Cucumbers 57
20. Low Sodium Dill Pickle Slices 57
21. Sugar-Free Sweet Pickle Slices 58
22. Low-sodium Sweet Pickle Slices 58

Refrigerator Recipes 59

23. Quick Sweet Radish Pickles 59
24. Cucumber and Onions Refreshing Pickles 60
25. Japanese Style Pickled Red Cabbage 61
26. Fennel and Orange Pickles 62
27. Pickled Red Onion and Lime 62

Pickling fruits recipes 63

28. Ginger Spiced Crabapples 63
29. Cinnamon Fig Pickles 64
30. Cinnamon Spiced Crabapples 65
31. Sweet Pickled Watermelon Rind 66
32. Pear Pickles 66
33. Sweet and Tangy Watermelon Rind Pickles 67
34. Pickled Cantaloupe with a Sweet and Tangy Flavor ... 68
35. Honey-Spiced Oranges 69

36. Tangy Peach Pickles 69

37. Pickled Plums with Red Onions 70

38. Bittersweet Spiced Plum Pickles 71

Quick Fresh-Pack Recipes 72

39. Pickled Ginger, Japanese Style 72

40. Cherries Pickled with Spices 73

41. Berry Pickle with a Sweet and Sour Taste 73

42. Strawberry Jam with Lavender and Honey 74

43. Rhubarb Pickles 74

44. Quick Grapes Pickles 75

45. Avocado Pickles 75

CHAPTER 10
Chutney—Relish—Salsa Recipes 76

Chutney 76

46. Apple Tomato Chutney 78

47. Cranberry Orange Chutney with a Tang 79

48. Apple Chutney with Sweet and Spicy Flavors 80

49. Pear Chutney 81

50. Kiwi and Peach Chutney with Spices 82

51. Fig and Apple Balsamic Chutney 83

52. Pumpkin and Cranberry Chutney with Spices 84

53. Rhubarb and Orange Chutney with a Tang 85

54. Jalapeño Pineapple Relish 86

55. Mixed Peppers Relish 87

Pickled Eggs 88

56. Eggs Pickled with Dill 88

57. Pineapple and Spicy Pickled Eggs 89

58. Pickled Eggs with Red Beet 90

Meat and Fish 91

59. Recipe for Canning Meat; Beef, Pork, and More 92

60. Canning Recipe for Poultry; Chicken, Turkey, and More 93

61. Canned Meatballs in Salsa 94

62. Canned Chili Con Carne 95

Seafood 96

63. Canned Fish Recipe: Trout, Salmon, Bluefish 97

64. Traditional Oyster Canning 98

65. Canned Tuna Recipe 99

66. Classic Shrimp Canning 100

CHAPTER 11
Fermenting Recipes 102

Guidelines for Fermentation 103

Preparation and Fermentation; Step-by-Step Recipes 105

Guide to Calculating Salt for Fermentation 106

Sauerkraut 107

   67. Classic Cabbage Sauerkraut 108

   68. Homemade Sauerkraut Made Easy 110

   69. Beet-Infused Sauerkraut 110

   70. Beetroot and Ginger Sauerkraut............................110

   71. Sauerkraut with Apple 111

   72. Carrot and Sauerkraut Mix 111

   73. Sauerkraut with Orange Flavor 111

   74. Fermented Tangy Coleslaw...................................112

   75. Turmeric-Ginger Pineapple Sauerkraut 112

Vegetables & Fruits Fermenting 113

   76. Fermented Dill Cucumber Pickles............................113

   77. Gingered Carrot Lacto-Fermented............................114

   78. Lacto-Fermented Turnips and Beets 114

   79. Onion Lacto-Fermented 115

   80. Fermented Radish Recipe 115

   81. Garlic Fermented in Honey..................................116

   82. Lemon Lacto-Fermented....................................117

   83. Cherry Tomatoes Fermented 118

   84. Red Cabbage and Mango Fermentation 119

   85. Plums Lacto-Fermented 120

   86. Fermented Mixed Berries 121

   87. Honey Fermented Plums 122

Kimchi 123

   88. Traditional Korean Baechu Kimchi 124

   89. Easy Kimchi Recipe 125

   90. Kimchi with Daikon Radish 126

   91. Korean Cucumber Kimchi 126

Miso & Tempeh 127

   92. Miso Made at Home 128

   93. Making Tempeh at Home 130

Condiments 132

   94. Spicy Mustard Fermented...................................132

   95. Cranberry Relish Fermented 133

   96. Tomato and Jalapeño Fermented Salsa 134

   97. Hot Sauce Lacto-Fermented.................................135

98. Worcestershire Sauce Made at Home..136

99. Ketchup Fermented at Home..137

Dairy and Bread 138

100. Recipe for Starting Sourdough...139

101. Classic Sourdough Bread..141

102. Starter for Gluten-Free Sourdough 143

103. Gluten-Free Sourdough Bread...144

Kefir: Uses and Maintenance.. 145

104. Recipe for Milk Kefir 148

105. Cheese from Milk Kefir..149

106. Tzatziki Made with Kefir..150

107. Mascarpone Cheese with Kefir 151

108. Making Butter at Home..152

Beverages... 153

109. Recipe for Water Kefir 153

110. Coconut Water Kefir Made at Home 154

Kombucha... 155

111. Kombucha Brewed at Home 157

112. Kombucha with Elderberry and Ginger 159

CHAPTER 12
FAQs and Problem Solving

FAQs and Problem Solving **160**

FAQ 160

Problems and Solutions... 161

CONCLUSION **166**

YOUR BONUS Food Preserving Planner........................ **167**

ALPHABETICAL RECIPE INDEX **169**

CONVERSION CHART **171**

RESOURCES **172**

INTRODUCTION

Welcome to a world of authentic flavors, culinary traditions, and a healthy approach to eating! My name is Sophie Magnant, and I am a chef from Louisiana with a deep passion for gardening and food preservation, especially through fermentation and pickling. I want to share with you not just the techniques I have honed over the years, but also a food philosophy that has the power to transform the way you live, eat, and conceive food.

In today's fast-paced world, finding time to buy fresh vegetables can become a real challenge. Here, pickling and fermentation emerge as valuable methods, which not only extend the life of our precious harvests but also allow maintaining not just a sufficient but also a creative and healthy food supply in your kitchen. These tradition-rich techniques invite you to rediscover the pleasure of homemade cooking, where every preserved ingredient becomes a testament to a love for authentic food and a life lived with intention and care.

In my first book, "Pickling and Fermenting Cookbook for Preppers," I will share with you all the secrets for healthy and effective food preservation. You will learn how to select the right vegetables and spices, prepare the ingredients, and ensure safety at every stage by aligning with food safety protocols. This approach not only ensures that the pickling and fermentation techniques are carried out with the utmost attention to healthfulness but also emphasizes that, while adhering to high standards, the proposed methodologies are designed to be universally applicable, making these practices accessible to anyone, anywhere. This includes managing temperatures and process stages to achieve delicious and nutritious dishes. Regardless of your experience level, whether you are an expert or a beginner, I will guide you step by step through this fascinating world, making food preservation a joyful and effortless part of your daily life.

I invite you to join me on this culinary adventure, where every preserved vegetable is not just an act of love towards ourselves and our planet, but also a step towards a future where we eat, live, and take care of our health more consciously and sustainably. Let's start this journey together, discovering how simple changes in our kitchen can lead to a healthier and happier life for us and for future generations.

CHAPTER 1
INTRODUCTION TO PICKLING AND FERMENTING AS FOOD PRESERVATION

Pickling and fermentation are two food preservation techniques increasingly gaining popularity in the culinary world. These techniques have ancient roots in many cultures and culinary traditions around the globe. But what precisely do these methods entail, and why are they deemed so significant?

In short, pickling involves immersing foods in an acidic solution, while fermentation entails the transformation of food sugars into lactic acid through the action of bacteria and yeast.

The rising popularity of these techniques can be attributed to their health and environmental benefits. They enable natural food preservation without resorting to synthetic additives, increasing the nutritional value by making vitamins and minerals more accessible. Moreover, pickling and fermentation are excellent strategies for minimizing food waste, extending the shelf life of produce, and ensuring a sustained, nutrient-rich food supply.

Beyond their practical advantages, these methods are a celebration of global culinary heritage, preserving the rich tapestry of food traditions from around the world.

In this guide, we'll unveil the secrets to producing high-quality, flavorful preserved foods. We'll cover various pickling and fermentation techniques, discuss their health benefits, and show you how to incorporate them into delightful recipes.

We'll also dive into the critical factors that ensure pickling and fermentation success, including the roles of temperature, time, and protection against oxygen and contaminants.

To inspire your culinary adventures, we've included a collection of modern, delicious recipes that showcase the versatility and appeal of pickling and fermentation. Get ready to embark on a journey that promises to enrich your diet and introduce you to the enduring legacy of these preservation methods.

History and Importance of Food Preservation Methods

Pickling and fermentation are ancient techniques of food preservation that have been used for millennia in various parts of the world, such as Mesopotamia, China, Europe, and the Middle East. They have been employed for a wide range of foods, including fruits, vegetables, meat, fish, and dairy products.

In Europe, fermented cabbage was a popular food during winter, and German sauerkraut is still highly regarded today as a side dish or condiment. In Asia, tea fermentation has been used to produce kombucha, while in the Middle East, pickling has been applied to olives.

Today, pickling and fermentation have become popular among those seeking to eat more healthily and sustainably. Due to their beneficial health properties and the fact that they enable natural food preservation without the use of artificial preservatives, pickling, and fermentation have become a growing food trend in recent years.

Difference between Pickling and Fermentation

To clarify the distinction and dispel any confusion, let's simplify the concepts of pickling and fermentation, despite their apparent similarities. The essence of pickling lies in submerging food in an acidic solution, typically brine, which imparts a tangy taste.

Fermentation, in contrast, relies on the action of natural bacteria to produce acids, which then impart a tangy taste to the food. This key difference underlines the unique processes each method employs to achieve its characteristic flavor.

Nurturing Gut Health through Fermented Foods

- **Improved Digestive Health**: Fermentation is a natural source of probiotics, the beneficial bacteria that play a crucial role in maintaining a healthy gut microbiome. This enhances digestion and the absorption of nutrients.
- **Enhanced Nutrient Absorption**: The fermentation process increases the bioavailability of vitamins and minerals in foods, making it easier for our bodies to absorb these essential nutrients.

- **Rich in B Vitamins and Vitamin K2**: Fermented foods are abundant in B vitamins and Vitamin K2, nutrients that bolster our immune system and protect against infections.
- **Lower Risk of Chronic Diseases:** The antioxidants and anti-inflammatory compounds in fermented foods contribute to a reduced risk of chronic conditions such as diabetes, heart disease, and certain cancers.
- **Blood Sugar Regulation**: Fermented foods can aid in stabilizing blood sugar levels by improving digestion and nutrient absorption.
- **Boosted Immune Function:** The probiotics generated through fermentation strengthen the immune system, enhancing the body's resistance to illness and promoting overall well-being.

Pickling and fermentation are not just culinary arts; they're gateways to refined taste experiences and substantial health benefits. These age-old methods not only enhance flavors but also enrich foods with beneficial bacteria, enzymes, and nutrients, offering a range of health advantages.

Fermented foods, loaded with probiotics, support the gastrointestinal tract, easing bloating and discomfort. Nutrient-dense staples like sauerkraut and kombucha boost the immune system, offering protection against heavy metals and inflammation. Thus, integrating fermented foods into your diet is a key strategy for overall health improvement, allowing you to enjoy a variety of flavors and reap significant health benefits.

The gut microbiota, a complex ecosystem in our gastrointestinal tract, is essential for digesting food, absorbing nutrients, and regulating the immune system. This vibrant community of microorganisms has a profound impact on our overall health, influencing mental well-being and playing a preventive role against chronic diseases such as diabetes and obesity.

Supporting a healthy gut microbiota is crucial, and one effective way to do this is through regular consumption of fermented foods like kefir, sauerkraut, and kombucha. These probiotic-rich foods promote a balanced and beneficial bacterial environment in the gut.

By incorporating fermented foods into your diet, you're taking a simple yet impactful step towards a healthier gut microbiota. Small dietary changes can make a big difference in the health and equilibrium of this complex microbial ecosystem within us.

CHAPTER 2

PICKLING

Basic Principles of Pickling

Are you curious about how to preserve your favorite vegetables and fruits, adding a delightful tang and extending their shelf life?

Pickling is a simple and satisfying method to transform fresh produce into a delectable, long-lasting treat. This guide will walk you through the basics of pickling, introducing you to this ancient technique that not only enhances flavor but also offers health benefits.

How Does Pickling Work?

At its core, pickling is a method of preserving food by immersing it in a solution of water, salt, and often vinegar, creating an environment where bacteria can't thrive. This process can be done in two main ways: using vinegar for a quick pickle or through fermentation, where natural bacteria ferment the food, producing lactic acid.

Different Pickling Methods

Vinegar Brine Pickling

This method is quick and straightforward, involving a mixture of vinegar, water, and salt, along with spices and herbs for added flavor. Foods pickled this way are submerged in the acidic brine, which prevents the growth of harmful bacteria and gives the pickles their characteristic sour taste. Ideal for beginners, this approach is versatile enough for a wide range of vegetables. It incorporates several sub-methods, often involving home canning techniques like water bath canning, which enables the preserved foods to remain edible for a year or two when stored in a cool, dry place.

Fermentation-Based Pickling

Fermentation-based pickling is a traditional approach that utilizes the natural process of lacto-fermentation, unfolding over weeks during which the product evolves in color, flavor, and texture. Salt added to vegetables draws out water, creating a brine that encourages the growth of beneficial bacteria. These microorganisms convert the sugars in the food into lactic acid, acting as a natural preservative, thereby naturally preserving the vegetables and enriching them with health-beneficial probiotics. This traditional method not only ensures the safety and quality of the finished product but also enhances its taste and nutritional properties.

Fresh-Pack or Quick Process Pickling

This method is a straightforward way to start pickling, using vinegar's acetic acid instead of relying on fermentation's lactic acid. It's suitable for almost any raw or lightly cooked vegetable. The process involves placing vegetables in jars and pouring over them a boiling mixture of vinegar, sugar, and spices. This quick pickling method needs only a short processing time and results in pickles that should be refrigerated and enjoyed within two weeks, making it ideal for small batches and immediate consumption.

Refrigerator or Freezer Pickling

Refrigerators or freezer pickles offer a swift method to preserve garden produce. This approach encourages creativity, providing a range of recipes suitable for various vegetables. However, it's important to note that these pickles are not shelf-stable and should be consumed within a month of storage in the refrigerator, ensuring freshness and optimal taste.

Other Pickled Products

Fruit Pickles

Fruit pickles feature whole or sliced fruits slow-cooked in sweet and tangy syrup made from vinegar or lemon juice, offering a unique blend of flavors.

Relishes and Chutneys

Relishes: A condiment made by chopping fruits and vegetables and cooking them in a spicy vinegar solution. Relishes enhance the flavor of various dishes, reflecting a wide range of culinary traditions across different cultures.

Chutneys: A versatile sauce made from a mix of aromatic herbs, flavorings, and chopped fruits or vegetables, slow-cooked with spices, onions, sugar, and vinegar. Each Indian region offers its unique chutneys, from spicy tomato to sweet coconut, complementing main dishes and enriching the dining experience.

Both relishes and chutneys provide a rich tapestry of tastes and aromas, easily customized to personal or regional preferences, making every meal a delightful experience.

USE FRESH INGREDIENTS: THE QUALITY OF YOUR PICKLES DEPENDS ON THE FRESHNESS OF THE PRODUCE YOU USE. FRESH, CRISP VEGETABLES WILL YIELD THE BEST RESULTS.

- *Keep everything clean:* Ensure all jars and utensils are sterilized to prevent contamination.
- *Experiment with flavors:* Don't hesitate to experiment with different spices, herbs, and vinegar types to find your favorite combinations.
- *Be Patient:* Especially with fermented pickles, the flavors develop over time. Allow your pickles to sit for at least a few weeks to mature.

Pickling is a fantastic way to preserve seasonal produce, reduce food waste, and add an exciting twist to your meals. Whether you prefer the quick and easy vinegar brine method or the traditional fermented approach, pickling opens up a world of culinary possibilities. With a little practice and patience, you can master the art of pickling, enjoying your homemade creations for months to come.

CHAPTER 3
PREPARATION FOR PICKLING

Selection of Products

When selecting ingredients for canning and pickling, it is important to choose high-quality varieties of fruits and vegetables specifically suited for this purpose.

- Tender vegetables
- Firm and ripe fruit, except for pears and peaches that can be slightly under-ripe
- Wax-coated pickling cucumbers are not suitable for pickling
- Thoroughly wash the produce
- Discard any items with mold
- Place in brine within 24 hours of harvest for the best quality
- Blossom end: Trim a 1/16-inch slice from the cucumber's blossom end as it contains enzymes that can lead to softening.

Selection of Ingredients

Salt

For pickling, it's crucial to use the right type of salt to ensure the quality and safety of your preserved foods. The best choice is pure granulated salt, known as canning or pickling salt, available in the canning aisle of most grocery stores.

Ensure the salt is free from anti-caking agents and iodine to prevent brine cloudiness and sediment formation.

Maintain the salt concentration as specified in recipes; altering it can affect preservation and safety.

Kosher salt, with its larger grains and lack of iodine, serves as a viable alternative for pickling.

Vinegar

- Vinegar plays a key role in pickling as a preservative, with white vinegar and cider vinegar being common choices. However, it's worth noting that cider vinegar might change the color of lighter pickles. For preserving the color of onions, cauliflower, and pears, white vinegar is recommended due to its clarity.
- Ensure the vinegar used has an acidity level of 5–6%, which is typical for commercial vinegars. Always verify the acidity on the product label to ensure safety. Diluting vinegar or using homemade varieties with uncertain acidity levels is discouraged.
- In cases where the pickles taste too acidic, a small amount of sugar can be added to balance the fla-

vor—typically, ¼ cup of white granulated sugar per 4 cups of vinegar, which won't compromise the pickle's safety.

- When preparing the vinegar solution for preservation, avoid prolonged boiling as the acetic acid (responsible for preservation) can evaporate, reducing its effectiveness.
- Remember, altering the ingredient proportions could affect the safety and quality of your pickled products, so it's essential to follow tested recipes closely.

Spices

- Best choice for fresh and whole spices to enhance the flavor and quality of your pickles.
- Avoid ground spices these can darken the pickle brine and create cloudiness.
- Keep spices in a cool place, around 70°F, in airtight containers to preserve their freshness.
- Enclose whole spices in a clean, white cloth or cheesecloth bag for easy removal before jar packing, ensuring clearer brine.

Fresh, whole spices are essential for clear, flavorful pickles, while ground spices may affect the appearance and clarity of the brine. Store spices properly and consider renewing your spice stock each pickling season to maintain peak aroma and effectiveness.

Sugar

- *Preferred type:* Use white granulated sugar unless a recipe specifically calls for brown sugar.
- *Caution when using substitutes:* Sugar alternatives are generally not advised due to potential bitterness and loss of sweetening power over time.
- *Purpose:* Beyond adding sweetness, sugar helps maintain the pickles' firmness and texture.

For pickling, traditional sugar is recommended to ensure desirable taste and texture, as substitutes may not yield the same results and could affect the pickles' quality over time.

Firming Agents

QUALITY INGREDIENTS: START WITH HIGH-QUALITY

INGREDIENTS TO AVOID THE NEED FOR CHEMICAL FIRMING AGENTS.

- *Ice water soak:* Immerse cucumbers in ice water for 4–5 hours to enhance their crispness.
- *Trimming:* Remove 1/16 inch from the blossom end of cucumbers to help firm them up.

The use of traditional firming agents like lime or alum is not recommended due to potential safety concerns. Simple practices such as soaking cucumbers in ice water or trimming the blossom end are effective and safe alternatives to achieve crispy pickles.

Using Lime for Firmness

- *Calcium benefit:* Lime's calcium content can improve pickle firmness but must be used carefully.
- *Correct type:* Only use food-grade pickling lime, avoiding agricultural or burnt lime.
- *Soaking procedure:* Soak cucumbers in a lime-water solution for 12–24 hours before brining, then thoroughly rinse and soak in fresh water three times to remove any excess lime, ensuring safety.

Careful handling and thorough rinsing are crucial when using lime to avoid health risks and ensure the pickles are safe for consumption.

Water Selection:

- *Quality matters:* Utilize drinking or purified water for pickling to ensure quality.
- *Softening hard water:* If hard water is your only option, boil it for 15 minutes and let it sit covered for 24 hours before decanting to use, or simply use distilled water as an alternative.

Choosing the right type of water is essential for preventing unwanted effects on the pickles, such as discoloration or improper fermentation. Soft or purified water is preferred to maintain the appearance and quality of the pickles.

Important Safety Tips

- *Maintain acidity levels:* For safety, it's crucial not to change the ratios of vinegar, food, or water specified in recipes.
- *Avoid botulism:* Adhering to correct proportions helps prevent the development of botulinum toxin.
- *Caution with unsealed jars:* Never consume food from jars that haven't been properly sealed or show signs of spoilage.

Equipment and Tools Required for Pickling

 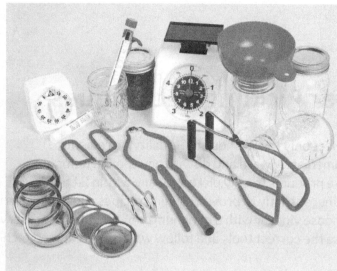

- Choose pots made of stainless steel, glass, aluminum, or enamel without chips for preparing your brine solution. It's important to steer clear of copper, brass, iron, or galvanized materials.
- A sizable water bath canner with a rack is essential to keep jars off the pot's bottom, ensuring even heating.
- Use quality glass jars, like Mason jars, that ensure a tight seal. Avoid reusing old jars that might not seal properly.
- Employ new two-piece sealing lids and bands for each batch to guarantee freshness.
- Essential tools include a funnel, jar lifter, bubble remover, and a magnetic tool for lid placement. These items are often sold in comprehensive pickling kits.
- Don't forget a reliable timer and a digital scale for precise measurements.

The selected pot should be deep enough to submerge jars by 1–2 inches in boiling water, facilitating proper sterilization. Precise measurement of ingredients using a digital scale is critical for the balance of salt and vinegar, adhering to tested recipes for safety and taste.

Purchase lids intended for near-term use to avoid the drying out of the sealant, which can affect the seal's integrity. While lids are single-use, metal screw bands can be reused if they remain undamaged and rust-free.

A vacuum seal, indicated by a depressed lid, signifies successful canning and preservation of your pickled goods.

CHAPTER 4

SAFE STORAGE METHODS AND PICKLING PROCESS

Proper Pickling Techniques

- Select only the freshest, top-quality ingredients.
- Immediately wash and discard any spoiled items.
- Use products freshly picked, ideally within 24 hours.
- Adhere strictly to proven pickling recipes and avoid altering ingredient ratios.
- Choose vinegar with a minimum of 5% acidity for preservation.
- Use the correct tools and follow water bath canning techniques diligently.

Storing Pickled Foods Safely

- Enhance preservation by adding acid, such as vinegar or lemon juice, to lower the pH.
- Employ salt in your brine to extract moisture and sugars, aiding in lactic acid formation that hinders spoilage.
- Apply water bath canning to prevent microbial growth, ensuring vegetables are safely preserved by adjusting their acidity for the water bath process.

Vinegar plays a crucial role by boosting food acidity and serving as a natural preservative, while salt in the brine not only preserves but also contributes to the pickling process by facilitating lactic acid formation. The water bath canning method seals the deal by eliminating harmful microorganisms, ensuring your pickled goods are safely stored and ready to enjoy.

Acidity Levels in Food Preservation

High acidity foods (pH below 4.6): This category includes fruits and pickled items. They can be effectively preserved using the water bath canning method. The high temperatures reached during this process are adequate to kill Clostridium botulinum bacteria cells, making the spores a non-issue.

Low acidity foods (pH above 4.6): Foods such as meats, vegetables, poultry, and fish fall into this group. They require a more robust preservation method to ensure safety. Utilizing a pressure canner allows these foods to be heated under pressure to temperatures high enough to destroy Clostridium botulinum spores, thereby preventing botulism.

This concise overview delineates the critical differences in preserving high and low-acidity foods, emphasizing the importance of appropriate canning methods to ensure food safety.

Guide to Pickle Processing Methods

Water bath canning:

Ideal for preserving high-acid foods, water bath canning involves heating water to 212°F (100°C) to eliminate molds, yeasts, and certain bacteria. This method safeguards the quality of pickles by preventing microbial growth and enzymatic changes that can affect flavor, color, and texture. Use standard jars with self-sealing lids, adjusting processing times based on the food's acidity and size.

Altitude considerations:

At elevations above 1,000 feet, water's boiling point drops. This requires adjustments in processing times for water bath canning to ensure all bacteria are effectively killed. For pressure canning, increased pressure compensates for lower boiling temperatures at high altitudes. To determine the correct adjustments, consult your local county Extension office or the Soil Conservation Service.

"Reliable recipes will guide you in making these adjustments for altitudes over 1,000 feet."

Guidelines for Low-Temperature Pasteurization

Specific use: This method should be applied exclusively as per the recipe's instructions. It's not universally applicable, especially for low-sodium pickles, due to their unique preservation needs.

Procedure: Begin by filling jars with room-temperature products. Then, pour the hot brine or liquid over the contents, ensuring it's heated to between 165–180°F (74–82°C) for optimal pasteurization. It's crucial to leave the correct headspace, remove any air bubbles, clean the jar rims, securely adjust the lids, and then process the jars at 180°F (82°C) for 30 minutes.

Temperature monitoring: A thermometer is indispensable in this process to accurately maintain the required temperature, as guessing can lead to under-processing.

Uniform processing time: The 30-minute processing time at 180°F (82°C) holds constant across all types of products and altitudes when using low-temperature pasteurization.

Caution: Proper adherence to the specified temperature is vital. Failure to do so can result in spoilage. This method is favored for its ability to preserve the texture of the product but demands careful attention to detail to prevent potential spoilage.

Note: Use this method only when specifically recommended by the recipe to ensure the safety and quality of the preserved food.

Jar and Lid Preparation for Canning

- **Inspection:** Before use, examine jars for any cracks or scratches and lids for imperfections in the sealing compound.
- **Cleaning:** Wash jars and screw bands thoroughly in hot, soapy water.
- **Sterilization:** Boil the jars for 10 minutes to sterilize them, then keep them and the lids warm until they are filled.
- **Lid selection:** Choose two-piece lids and avoid reusing them, as they are designed for single use only.

It's essential to clean and pre-sterilize jars to ensure the safety of canned goods. Be sure to use lids within a year of purchase to prevent the sealing compound from drying out, which could affect the seal's effectiveness. While lids are for one-time use due to the potential degradation of the sealing compound, screw bands may be reused if they remain free from damage and rust.

Key notes:

- **Sterilization and keeping jars warm are critical steps before filling them with hot contents.**
- **Use new lids for each canning session to guarantee a secure seal.**
- **Clean screw bands with hot, soapy water without the need for boiling.**

Canning Packing Techniques

Fruits and vegetables can be canned using either the raw or hot pack method. Preheating the produce before packing enhances both color and flavor, particularly with water bath canning. Regardless of the method, ensure sufficient liquid is added to cover the produce, preventing discoloration and off-flavors. Generally, you'll need **½ to 1 ½ cups of liquid for each one-liter jar.**

Raw Pack Method

- **Pack raw, uncooked produce into jars.**
- **Pour boiling liquid over the produce to cover it.**
- **Firmly pack fruits and most vegetables as they will shrink during processing.**
- **Starchy vegetables that expand during processing should be packed more loosely.**

In raw packing, it's crucial to fill the jars with raw food without crushing it, and then cover it with hot liquid. Ensure you remove any air bubbles, secure the correct headspace, clean the jar rims, attach lids, adjust the rings, and process.

Hot Pack Method

- **Fill jars with precooked hot food and boiling liquid.**
- **Pack the food relatively loosely since it has already shrunk from cooking.**
- **Ensure the cooking liquid adequately covers the produce.**

The hot pack method, recommended for most foods, involves cooking the produce before canning. This approach requires fewer jars, minimizes food floating, preserves color and flavor better, and makes packing easier due to the food's softness. Always use the hot pack method if specified by the recipe.

Important: Always adhere to the recipe's specified packing method for the best results.

Filling Jar

- Start by filling the sterilized jars with your prepared product, and pouring in liquid according to the recipe's instructions.
- Maintain a ½-inch space from the top of the jar to allow for expansion, known as headspace.
- Eliminate air bubbles by gently stirring with a non-metallic spatula.
- Wipe the jar rims with a clean, damp cloth or paper towel to ensure a clean sealing surface.
- Use a magnetic lid lifter to place the lids on the jars carefully, then secure them lightly with your fingertips until just tight, avoiding over-tightening which can compromise the seal.
- After cooling, remove the screw bands to prevent them from sticking or rusting.

Control Headspace

- The gap between the food and the lid varies ¼ inch for jams and jellies, ½ inch for pickles, fruits, and tomatoes, and 1–1¼ inches for items in pressure canners.
- Correct headspace is crucial for ensuring a secure seal. Too much or too little can lead to sealing failures.

Headspace is vital for food expansion during heating and creating a vacuum as jars cool. Adhering to the recipe's specified headspace is key for a successful seal, as incorrect headspace can lead to air retention or prevent the jar from sealing effectively.

Canning Process for Pickles

Carefully position jars using a jar lifter onto the canner rack without tilting them. Ensure the water in the canner is already at 180°F (82°C) for hot pack and 140°F (60°C) for raw pack before introducing the jars.

Adhering to processing times

Be mindful that each type of food requires a specific processing time, which can also vary with jar size.

An inadequate processing period can lead to spoilage and potential health risks.

It's essential to follow precise instructions for the processing time based on the food type and jar size during canning. Insufficient processing may result in food spoilage or unsafe consumption. Canning is crucial for eliminating harmful bacteria and inactivating enzymes that affect food's ripening and color, ensuring the food remains safe and retains its quality.

Cooling and Sealing Process for Canned Jars

Cooling jars

- After canning, use a jar lifter to carefully remove the jars without tilting them. Place them on a clean towel or a heat-resistant surface like a plastic or wooden cutting board away from drafts to cool.

Checking jar seals

- Let the jars cool undisturbed for 12–24 hours before inspecting the seals.
- Once sealed, remove the ring bands, clean the jar's sealing surface and threads, then store the jars without bands in a cool, dark, and dry place.

- Unsealed jars should be reprocessed immediately with new lids and a water bath canner or stored in the refrigerator to be used within a week.

Seal verification

- Canning deactivates enzymes and removes oxygen, preserving the food's quality by creating a vacuum inside the jars. This vacuum keeps liquids in and air and microorganisms out. Seal integrity can be checked through several methods:

1. Sound: Listen for a distinct popping sound as the jars cool, indicating the formation of a vacuum seal.
2. Visual and touch: Check that the lids have curved downward or inward and do not move when pressed.
3. Tap test: Tap the center of the lid with a metal spoon. A sealed jar will produce a clear ringing sound, while an unsealed jar will emit a dull thud.

These steps ensure that the canned goods are properly sealed and stored, maintaining their quality and safety for future enjoyment.

Guidelines for Storing Home-Canned Foods

- After ensuring the jars are sealed, remove and discard the ring bands.
- Wipe the lid and jar surface to clean any residue.
- Clearly label each jar with its contents and the date of canning.
- Store in a consistently cool, dark, and dry area, away from any direct light or heat sources to prevent spoilage.
- Aim to use canned goods within one year for optimal quality and nutrition.

Identifying Spoilage in Canned Goods

Be vigilant for any of these signs that indicate food spoilage:

- Lids that are bulging or lids that have lost their seal
- Changes in the food's color that appear unnatural
- The presence of increasing air bubbles within the jar
- Striations or trails of dried food on the inside of the jar that indicate leakage
- Any leakage of liquid from the jar
- Off smells or odors that are not typical of the canned item
- Mold growth, which may appear as cotton-like formations, in various colors (white, blue-black, or green) on the food's surface or underneath the lid

Safety Precautions

- Do not taste: Avoid tasting the contents from jars that are unsealed or exhibit signs of spoilage.
- To inspect a jar, hold it at eye level and rotate it to check for any dried food streaks or other indicators of spoilage mentioned above.
- Upon opening, be alert to any signs of liquid leakage, unusual odors, or visible mold.
- If deterioration is detected, dispose of the jar's contents safely. For low-acid foods, it's recommended to first boil the jar and its contents for 30 minutes to neutralize any potential toxins, then cool and discard securely to prevent health risks to humans and animals.

These practices ensure the safety and quality of home-canned foods, protecting against foodborne illnesses.

Step-by-Step Guide to Water Bath Canning

Follow these detailed steps to ensure safe and successful water bath canning:

1. Sterilization: Wash jars and lids thoroughly, then boil them for 10 minutes to sterilize. Keep jars warm until use. Remember, lids should be new and bands should not be heated.
2. Canner preparation: Fill your water bath canner with the appropriate amount of water and preheat to 180°F (82°C) or 140°F (60°C).
3. Ingredient preparation: Prepare your ingredients according to a trusted recipe.
4. Packing jars: Dry the jars before packing them with food. Use a funnel to add liquids, leaving a ½-inch headspace at the top.
5. Air removal: Use a non-metal spatula to gently remove any air bubbles from the jars.
6. Cleaning rims: Wipe jar rims with a clean, damp paper towel to ensure a clean sealing surface.
7. Lid placement: Place lids on jars, securing gently with fingertips, then screw on the metal bands until snug.
8. Canner loading: Use a jar lifter to place jars on the canner rack. If needed, add more water so it covers 1–2 inches above the jars. Avoid pouring water directly onto the lids.
9. Boiling: Ensure the water reaches a boil 212°F (100°C) before starting the timer.

10. Processing time: Process the jars in boiling water for the time specified by your recipe, and adjusting for altitude as necessary.
11. Jar removal: Carefully lift jars from the canner without tilting them, placing them on a cloth to cool, and ensuring air circulates in each jar.
12. Cooling period: Allow jars to rest undisturbed for 12–24 hours before checking seals.
13. Seal test: Listen for a popping sound as jars cool, indicating a proper seal.
14. Post-process: Remove bands, clean jars, and label with contents and date.

If a jar hasn't been sealed properly (the lid can be pressed down), refrigerate it and use it within two weeks. Store sealed jars in a cool, dark place and consume within a year for the best quality. Always inspect and smell contents upon opening; if in doubt, discard the product.

Detailed Steps for the Pressure Canner Process

3

4

10

Pressure canning is essential for safely canning low-acid foods such as meats, vegetables, poultry, and seafood. Always adhere to the specific instructions provided by your pressure canner's manufacturer and ensure that dial-gauge canners are tested yearly for accuracy.

1. Water preparation: Begin by adding 2–3 inches of hot water to your canner, verifying there's adequate water for the entire process.
2. Jar preparation: Ready your jars according to standard packing methods, ensuring correct headspace and sealing after removing any air bubbles and cleaning the rims.
3. Canner loading: Place the prepared jars on the canner's rack to allow steam circulation. Open the lid and vent the steam for 10 minutes to evacuate the air, crucial for achieving accurate temperature control during canning.
4. Sealing and pressurizing: Seal the vent with the canner's weight or valve. For dial-gauge canners, bring the pressure up to 8 lb, then adjust heat to stabilize pressure. Begin timing once the desired pressure level is reached. For weighted-gauge canners, heat until the weight gently rocks or jiggles 2–3 times per minute, marking the start of your processing time.

5. Heat management: Maintain steady pressure, adjusting the heat as necessary. Never attempt to reduce pressure by opening the vent or removing the weight.
6. Processing time: If pressure drops below the recommended level at any point, return to the correct pressure and restart the timer, using the full processing duration.
7. Cooling: After processing, remove the canner from heat and let pressure return to zero naturally, which can take 30–45 minutes or longer, depending on the canner size. Do not rush this process.
8. Depressurization: Wait until the canner fully depressurizes. Modern canners will indicate this with a safety lock feature; older models require manual checking.
9. Opening the canner: Once depressurized, open the vent, wait another 10 minutes, then carefully open the lid away from you to avoid steam.
10. Removing jars: Carefully lift jars out of the canner, placing them on a rack or towel with space in between to cool without touching.
11. Cooling jars: Allow jars to cool undisturbed for 12–24 hours without adjusting the lids.

As a conclusion to the process, this guide underscores the critical steps necessary for successful pressure canning. Emphasizing safety, precision, and the imperative of adhering to the manufacturer's guidelines and specified processing times, it aims to ensure the highest standards of food safety and quality are maintained. Following these directions carefully will help preserve your foods safely, extending their shelf life while keeping their nutritional value intact.

CHAPTER 5
FERMENTATION

The Art of Fermentation

Fermentation stands apart from the vinegar and brine preservation methods discussed in the preceding chapter. This unique process leverages lactic acid, produced through lactic fermentation by Lactobacilli bacteria naturally found on vegetable surfaces, to preserve pickles.

The cornerstone of this method, lactic acid fermentation, not only preserves vegetables but also imbues them with several health benefits. In contrast to pickles made with vinegar and brine, fermented pickles offer a distinct flavor and aroma that arise directly from the fermentation process, without any need for added vinegar, sugar, or citrus. This method also enriches the pickles with beneficial live bacteria and probiotics, supporting gut health.

"Fermentation is a delicate dance, where logic and science lead with grace, guided not solely by instinct and intuition, but by a harmonious blend

of precision and wonder."

Addressing food spoilage, often caused by bacterial growth, fermentation introduces an acidic environment conducive only to specific bacteria, like Lactobacillus, thereby preventing spoilage. This principle underlies the production of lacto-fermented vegetables.

Creating lacto-fermented vegetables involves submerging them in saltwater brine, allowing them to ferment over a period that varies according to the recipe and taste preferences. This period allows natural microorganisms to convert sugars into lactic acid and other beneficial compounds. These compounds lower the pH, making the environment inhospitable to harmful bacteria, molds, and wild yeasts, thus preserving the vegetables and ensuring their safety.

To ensure vegetables remain submerged in the brine, fermentation weights and vessels, such as crocks, are used. The salt in the brine extracts water from the vegetables, facilitating the production of carbon dioxide, ethanol, and lactic acid, creating a perfect habitat for beneficial bacteria and probiotics. This makes lacto-fermented pickles a particularly healthy choice.

Sauerkraut is a renowned example of a lacto-fermented pickle, with classic deli-style dill pickles and barrel-aged pickles also popular. Making lacto-fermented pickles can be surprisingly simple, especially with a fermenting crock or vessel at home. From sauerkraut to kimchi, this single vessel can produce a variety of fermented delights.

Entering the world of fermentation can be one of the most exciting things you will ever experience, whether you're running a farm or looking to balance your commitments between home and work, optimizing your time. This adventure will offer you the opportunity to preserve your foods, enriching your family's diet throughout the year and adding a special touch to your routine. It will be an exhilarating experience that will make your life even more fulfilling, creating a harmonious and satisfying environment for yourself and the people you care about.

Benefits of Fermented Foods

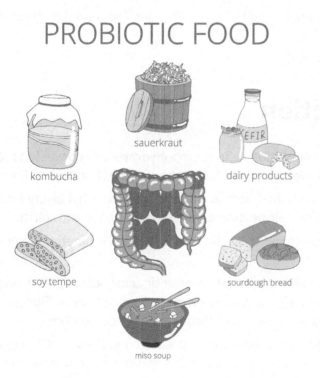

PROBIOTIC FOOD

kombucha

sauerkraut

KEFIR

dairy products

soy tempe

sourdough bread

miso soup

Fermentation is a process that can be applied to almost all raw and organic foods, resulting in products that are both tasty and beneficial for health. Here is a combined list of common and healthy fermented foods to include in your diet:

- **Yogurt and Kefir**: Produced from fermented milk, rich in probiotics, excellent for gut health.
- **Kombucha:** A tea-based fermented beverage, known for its probiotic benefits.
- **Sauerkraut and Kimchi:** Cabbage-based ferments, are known for their probiotic properties and high vitamin content.
- **Pickles:** Cucumbers fermented in a water and salt solution, famous for their crunchiness and flavor.
- **Miso, Tempeh, and Natto:** Soy-based fermented products, are beneficial for digestive health and rich in proteins.
- **Fermented Rye Bread:** Offers an alternative source of fermented grains.
- **Fermented Cheeses:** Such as cheddar and gouda, are beneficial for gut health.

- **Fermented Beverages:** Like beer and wine, produced through fermentation, though they contain alcohol.

These foods offer a wide range of health benefits, such as aiding digestion and providing essential nutrients. Regular inclusion in the diet can significantly improve overall well-being.

Basic Principles of Fermentation

The principles of preserving food through fermentation involve:

Sanitization: It is important to sanitize the equipment and surfaces that will come into contact with the fermented food, to prevent contamination from harmful bacteria.

Acidification: During fermentation, beneficial bacteria metabolize the sugars present in the food, producing organic acids that lower the pH of the food. This prevents the growth of harmful bacteria and the spoilage of the food.

Oxygen removal: Fermentation occurs in an anaerobic environment, without oxygen. This prevents the growth of aerobic bacteria that require oxygen to survive.

Temperature control: It is important to maintain the food at an appropriate temperature for the type of fermentation being used, to ensure a healthy and safe fermentation process.

Selection of beneficial bacteria: For a healthy and safe fermentation, it is important to use the beneficial bacteria that naturally occur in the food or have been added through a starter culture, such as yeast or lactobacillus. This approach guarantees a stable and reliable process of fermentation.

Fermentation is a wonderful and ancient method of keeping our food fresh and tasty. It's all about working with nature, using some cool tricks like lowering the pH with acids, keeping air out, finding the perfect temperature, picking the right friendly microbes, and keeping everything clean. This magic combination not only keeps food good for a long time but also enhances its flavor and makes it easier on the stomach.

So, in a nutshell, fermentation is this awesome, eco-friendly, and delicious approach to food preservation that's worth exploring and embracing in our kitchens today.

It's like a culinary treasure trove waiting to be rediscovered!

Various Types of Fermentation

Lactic fermentation: It is the most common form of fermentation, where carbohydrates are converted into lactic acid by lactic acid bacteria. This technique is used to produce foods like yogurt, sauerkraut, and kimchi.

Alcoholic fermentation: In this form of fermentation, carbohydrates are converted into ethyl alcohol and carbon dioxide by yeast. It is used in the production of alcoholic beverages such as beer, wine, and spirits.

Acetic fermentation: Here, alcohol is converted into acetic acid by acetic acid bacteria. This method is used in the production of vinegar.

Mixed fermentation: Mixed fermentation involves the use of a combination of lactic acid bacteria, yeast, and/or acetic acid bacteria to achieve a more complex fermentation and a richer, more nuanced flavor. This technique is used to produce foods like sourdough bread, aged cheeses, and certain types of cured meats.

There are many variations of fermentation for the production of fermented foods around the world. However, for our pickling food preservation, we will focus on the three most common variations mentioned above.

Spontaneous Fermentation vs. Starter Cultures

In the realm of fermentation, there are two main paths to follow: spontaneous fermentation and the use of starter cultures. Each method offers unique benefits and caters to different fermentation goals.

Spontaneous Fermentation

This method relies on the microorganisms naturally present in the ingredients and the environment. By creating favorable conditions, such as adding salt to cabbage to make sauerkraut, the growth of beneficial bacteria rich in probiotic is encouraged.

Fermentation with Starter Cultures

Utilizing starter cultures involves introducing specific microorganisms to the ferment. This controlled addition gives these microbes an immediate advantage, allowing them to quickly adjust the environment to benefit their proliferation. Starter cultures are particularly useful for achieving consistent results and can be crucial for fermenting foods with high sugar content, where the risk of undesirable microbial competition is higher.

Do You Need Starter Cultures?

While commercial starter cultures are available and can be beneficial, they aren't strictly necessary for all types of fermentation. Lactic acid bacteria, essential for lactic acid fermentation, are ubiquitous in nature, and often present on the surfaces of fresh produce and in the air. Creating the right conditions is often suffices for spontaneous fermentation to occur.

In summary, the choice between spontaneous fermentation and using starter cultures depends on your specific fermentation project, desired outcomes, and whether consistency or experimenting with natural processes is the goal.

Lactic Fermentation

Lactic fermentation is a fascinating natural process where sugars in fruits and vegetables are transformed into lactic acid and carbon dioxide by lactic acid bacteria, such as various Lactobacillus strains. These beneficial bacteria are ubiquitous, found on the surface of plants, floating in the air, and even residing on our skin. In the right conditions, Lactobacillus species thrive, out-competing other microorganisms and producing lactic acid, which acts as a natural preservative, enhancing the food's flavor and extending its shelf life.

The Preservative Power of Lactic Acid

Lactic acid is a potent, natural preservative. It creates an acidic environment that deters harmful microorganisms, including bacteria, yeasts, and molds. The low pH environment it fosters is hostile to pathogens, making the food safe for consumption and providing a natural alternative to chemical preservatives. The bacteria driving this fermentation process are safe for health, positioning lactic acid fermentation as a preferred method for preserving food.

CHAPTER 6

STARTING YOUR FERMENTATION PROJECT

Essential Fermentation Tools and Equipment

Starting your fermentation journey—whether it's with sauerkraut, pickles, or other veggies—requires gathering a few key tools. It's crucial to clean these tools thoroughly with hot, soapy water before you begin. Here's a simplified list of what you need:

1. **Cutting board:** Essential for chopping your vegetables.
2. **Vegetable slicer:** Use knives, mandolins, or food processors to slice your veggies evenly.
3. **Rounded pestle:** Ideal for crushing and juicing veggies like cabbage or carrots.
4. **Large mixing bowl:** Select glass or stainless steel to mix your ingredients.
5. **Starter culture (optional):** Use whey, kefir grains, or commercial starters to jumpstart fermentation.
6. **Fermentation container:** Your choice of vessel will greatly impact your fermentation project.
7. **Digital scale:** Ensures accurate measurements of ingredients and salt.

Selecting Your Fermentation Vessel

The container you choose is crucial for your fermentation. Options vary from simple glass jars to elaborate ceramic crocks. Here's a brief guide to help you pick:

- **Glass jars:** Great for small batches. Wide-mouth Mason jars, ranging from half-pint to 1-gallon sizes, are versatile and easy to use.
- **Airlock lids:** These lids prevent air entry but allow gases to escape, simplifying fermentation.
- **Glass jars with airlock systems**: An affordable option that keeps out oxygen and lets gases out, reducing mold risk.
- **Fermentation kits:** These come with vented lids or airlocks, making the process easier.
- **Ceramic crocks:** Best for large batches. Choose a high-quality, glazed crock and avoid plastic to prevent chemical contamination.

For beginners, pint-sized mason or ball jars are recommended for small-scale experiments. It's important to keep veggies submerged in brine to prevent mold.

Weighting and Covering

Ensuring your sauerkraut and other vegetables remain submerged in brine and protected from the air is key for successful fermentation. Here's how to effectively weigh down and cover your ferments:

- **Fermentation weights:** Utilize glass or ceramic weights to keep everything underwater, minimizing oxygen exposure and preventing overflow.
- **Smaller jar technique:** Place a smaller, water-filled jar inside the fermentation container as a makeshift weight.
- **Food-safe bags:** Fill these with brine to act as weights. Make sure to use bags that are intended for food storage, not trash bags.
- **Plate method:** A ceramic or glass plate can be placed inside the container; add a sealed jar filled with water on top for extra weight. Ensure that the vegetables are submerged under 1–2 inches of brine.
- **Floating trap**: A cabbage leaf on top can act as a barrier, keeping smaller bits from floating to the surface.
- **Cloth cover:** Cover the ferment with a cloth and secure it with a rubber band to protect against dust and insects, while still allowing the ferment to breathe.

Quality Control Tools

For anyone wanting to improve their fermentation, precise tools are key. They help monitor and control the process, leading to better and more consistent results. Using these tools makes it easier to achieve high-quality fermentation every time.

- **Acidity monitoring:** Use pH strips or meters to keep an eye on the acidity level of your ferment, ensuring it's within the safe and desired range.
- **Temperature checks:** A reliable thermometer helps maintain the optimal fermentation temperature.
- **Keeping records:** Documenting each step in a notebook is invaluable. Note temperatures, pH levels, and any adjustments made during the process to refine and replicate successful batches.

These tools and techniques offer a comprehensive approach to managing the fermentation environment, ensuring your vegetables ferment safely and deliciously. Remember, detailed tracking is the secret to mastering the art of fermentation!

Safety and Basic Techniques

1. **Preparation:** Begin by rinsing the vegetables with filtered water, ensuring they remain raw. Slice all vegetables, leaving hot peppers for later.
2. **Mixing:** In a large bowl, combine the vegetables, adding salt to taste. Use your hands or a pounding tool to extract juices, which helps in the fermentation process.
3. **Starter culture (optional):** Enhance fermentation by adding a starter culture like whey, kefir grains, or a freeze-dried culture.
4. **Spicing it up:** Finely chop hot peppers, seeds removed, and add to the mixture. Handle with care to avoid skin irritation.
5. **Jar preparation:** Transfer the mixture to a glass jar, leaving at least 3 inches of space at the top. Ensure the vegetables are fully submerged in their juice by compressing them and using a weight.
6. **Sealing and storage:** Seal the jar with a specialized lid to prevent insect intrusion, allow gas to escape, and minimize oxygen exposure. Store in a dark, room-temperature spot.

Fermentation Time and Temperature Control

- **Duration:** Fermentation can take from 2 to 21 days. Monitor the process, adjusting for salt quantity, the use of starter cultures, ambient temperature, and personal taste preferences. The goal is to achieve a tangy or spicy flavor, indicating readiness.
- **Temperature:** Keep fermentation temperatures between 60°–70°F (15–21°C) for the best results.

Checking Progress

- Regularly taste and check that the vegetables remain submerged. Once the desired flavor is achieved, you can either move the jar to the fridge or let it ferment longer in a cooler spot for deeper flavors.

Storing Fermented Vegetables

1. **Short-term storage (4–6 Weeks):** Store in a cellar or refrigerator to slow fermentation and enhance flavor.

2. **Salt concentration for long-term storage:**

- **1–2% Salt:** Suitable for up to 4–9 months in the refrigerator.
- **2% Salt:** Keeps well in a cool, dark place like a cellar for at least 3 months, ensuring vegetables are submerged in brine.

Important Tips

- Ensure cleanliness and sanitation from the start to avoid contamination.
- Always make sure vegetables are submerged in brine to prevent mold and spoilage.
- Adapt salt levels and fermentation time based on personal taste and desired preservation length.

By grasping the essential conditions required for lacto-fermentation, you have the flexibility to ferment a wide variety of vegetables using two primary methods: creating brine naturally from the vegetables' juices or adding saltwater brine.

Self-Brining and Added-Brine Approaches

Diving into the world of fermentation, two fundamental approaches stand out: self-brining and added-brine methods. Each technique caters to different types of vegetables and desired textures, offering a versatile range of flavors for your fermentation projects.

Self-Brining Fermentation

This technique is perfect for fresh, moisture-rich vegetables. When salt is added to these vegetables, it naturally extracts water, forming a natural brine. To facilitate this process, the vegetables should be finely chopped or grated to increase the surface area, allowing for more effective brine extraction.

This method is ideal for making classics like sauerkraut, spiced grated carrots, or zucchini salsa. Simply mix your chosen veggies with salt, let them sit to release their juices, forming a brine, and ensure they are completely submerged. If the vegetables don't release enough liquid, an added brine (as described below) can be introduced to cover them adequately.

Added-Brine Fermentation

When working with vegetables that don't lend themselves to grating or fine chopping—think whole cucumbers or chunky carrot sticks—adding a prepared brine is the way to go. This involves creating a saltwater solution, typically using 3 tbsp of sea salt per quart of water, to cover the veggies, ensuring they stay submerged in an oxygen-free environment that promotes lactic acid bacteria growth. This method is versatile, and suitable for a broad array of vegetables like cucumbers, peppers, tomatoes, celery, and more, streamlining the preparation process and allowing for larger cuts of vegetables.

Choosing Your Method

The choice between self-brining and added-brine methods depends on the vegetables at hand and your personal preference for texture and flavor. Even traditionally self-brined vegetables like cabbage can be fermented in large pieces using the added-brine method. By experimenting with both techniques, you can enjoy a wide spectrum of fermented foods, enriching your diet with an array of probiotic-rich, flavorful options.

Preparing Vegetables for Fermentation

Embarking on vegetable fermentation requires understanding key principles, such as identifying when vegetables are fully fermented and the importance of leaving them at room temperature initially, without refrigeration.

A vital skill in this journey is learning the correct way to prepare vegetables, as the preparation method greatly affects the fermentation outcome, influencing both the ingredients and techniques needed for a superior product. The main preparation methods are Grating, Chopping, and Slicing, each impacting the fermentation steps that follow.

- **Grating:** Typically done with a food processor or a coarse grater, grating is suitable for harder or crispier vegetables. Examples of vegetables that are good candidates for grating include carrots, radishes, turnips, beets, cucumbers, zucchini, and cabbage. Grating creates the largest surface area among preparation techniques, allowing salt to penetrate more quickly, draw out moisture effectively, and create a natural brine for fermentation.
- **Chopping:** Cut vegetables into small to large pieces, akin to chopping onions. The size of the chop can affect fermentation time, with recipes often specifying the needed dimensions. Chopped vegetables like eggplants, asparagus, green beans, bell peppers, cucumbers, zucchini, and carrots, ferment slower than grated or thinly sliced ones, as the salt and water brine take longer to penetrate larger pieces.
- **Slicing:** increases surface area, aiding in quicker salt penetration and brine formation, beneficial for vegetables like cabbage used in sauerkraut. However, some vegetables may need added brine to ferment properly. Sliced vegetables, such as cabbage, cucumbers, zucchini, peppers, and celery, have a moderate fermentation time, providing flexibility for storage or extended fermentation periods.

In recipes suggesting grating or mincing, it's crucial to adapt based on the vegetable's texture, possibly adding brine if needed. Each method offers different advantages, influencing the fermentation speed and ease of preparation.

CHAPTER 7
MONITORING, STORAGE, AND TROUBLESHOOTING

Monitoring Temperature and Time

Temperature and time are critical elements in the fermentation process. Maintaining the required infusion temperature and adhering to the times specified in your recipe are essential aspects to ensure food safety. According to the "Food Protection 2020" report, it has been observed that lightly fermented or minimally acidified plant products have contributed to foodborne illnesses and various outbreaks.

In many of these situations, the issue has often been associated with acidified vegetables and products like kimchi. Maintaining the correct temperature is crucial for safely and effectively preparing fermented foods. This allows the food to undergo healthy fermentation while simultaneously destroying any harmful pathogens. Most products are fermented at specific temperature and time intervals as part of the fermentation process:

FOOD	TEMPERATURE RANGE	LENGTH
Cucumbers	70–75°F 55–65°F	3–4 weeks 5–6 weeks
Cabbage	70–75°F 60–65°F	3–4 weeks 5–6 weeks
Kimchi	40°F 68°F	3–4 days 1–2 days
Fruit	50–59°F	2–6 weeks
Kombucha	68–72°F	12 days minimum

Ideal temperature range: 70–75°F with a fermentation time of 3–4 weeks.

At 60–65°F, fermentation will take longer, typically 5–6 weeks.

Avoid temperatures above 75°F, as they can lead to spoilage.

Kimchi: Ferments at room temperature for 1–2 days or in the refrigerator for 3–4 days.

Fruit: Ferments at cooler temperatures and progresses faster due to its natural sugar content.

Kombucha: Avoid direct sunlight or outdoor exposure to prevent high temperatures. It takes from 12 days to 1 month to ferment.

Simplified Guide to Monitoring pH:

Monitoring the pH level is crucial for the safety and successful fermentation of vegetables. Here's a streamlined approach to ensure your fermented foods are safe and delicious:

pH Goals

Initial phase: Aim to lower the pH from around 7.0 (neutral) to below 5.2 within the first 24 hours of fermentation.

Secondary phase: Further reduce the pH to 4.6 or lower within the next 24 hours, aiming for a final pH drop to 4.0 for optimal safety.

How to Test pH

Daily testing: Take 2–3 brine samples from each container daily. Continue until the pH is consistently below 4.6.

Weekly checks: Once the desired pH is achieved, switch to weekly testing to monitor stability and flavor development.

Tools: Use a calibrated pH meter initially, then pH test strips once the pH falls below 4.0.

Temperature and time: Flavor development varies with temperature. Expect a 3–4-week process at 68–75°F, or 5–6 weeks at 60–65°F. Keep an eye out for spoilage, particularly in low-salt ferments or temperatures above 75°F.

Special Considerations for Kimchi

Rapid Testing: For kimchi, which ferments faster, test the pH every 12 hours at room temperature (68–72°F) for the first 2 days, or daily for 4 days if fermenting in the refrigerator at 40°F.

Fermentation Maintenance

Check your ferment daily for the first week to ensure the brine level is adequate. If it's low, add a diluted salt solution (1 tbsp salt in 2 cups water). After the first week, additional brine adjustments shouldn't be necessary.

It is important to carefully monitor the fermentation process and ensure that safety parameters are met before consuming the fermented food.

CHAPTER 8

SIGNS YOUR FERMENTED VEGETABLES ARE READY

Understanding When Fermented Vegetables Are Ready for Consumption

Embarking on the fermentation journey can be both exciting and a bit daunting, especially when it comes to recognizing when your fermented vegetables are perfectly ready to be enjoyed. To ensure safety and optimal taste, fermented foods should meet certain conditions before consumption:

Achieve food safety standards: This often means reaching a specific pH level that signifies a safe, acidic environment where harmful microorganisms cannot thrive.

Be dominated by beneficial microorganisms: The fermentation environment should be fully colonized by safe, beneficial strains of bacteria.

It's important to note that a quick fermentation process of just 2–3 days is not recommended. Such a short time frame does not allow for the necessary microbial competition and colonization to occur. Properly fermented vegetables usually reach their ideal state within 7–10 days, though this can vary based on temperature, the type of vegetable, and added ingredients.

Initial Stages of Fermentation: A Delicate Balance

The beginning of the fermentation process is critical, involving a battle for dominance among various microorganisms. With time, beneficial bacteria take over, creating a safe and stable product. Traditionally, fermenting took place in cool environments, such as cellars, which naturally extended the fermentation period. Today, recommendations often suggest a fermentation period of 3–10 days before refrigeration, but the fermenting activity continues, slowly evolving and enhancing the flavor over time.

Signs Your Fermented Vegetables Are Ready

Bubbles: The presence of bubbles in the brine or a fizzy taste indicates active fermentation by lactic acid bacteria—a positive sign.

Smell: Upon opening your fermentation vessel, a sour, tangy aroma should greet you. An off-putting smell, however, might mean the batch has spoiled.

Taste: Sampling is key. The vegetables should taste pleasantly sour if they're ready. Remember, fermentation progresses faster in warmer conditions.

Tips for Fermentation Newbies

Early signs such as a thin layer on the brine or vegetables floating to the top are normal but require vigilance.

In warmer climates, a few days at room temperature may be sufficient before refrigeration; in cooler climates, a week or more may be needed.

After observing initial fermentation signs, wait an additional 2–3 days in cooler climates and 1–2 days in warmer ones before refrigerating.

Trust your senses. Your sense of smell and taste are invaluable tools in determining when your ferment is ready for cold storage.

This guide aims to demystify the fermentation process, making it more accessible to beginners and emphasizing the key indicators of readiness for refrigeration. By paying attention to these signs, you'll be able to confidently enjoy your homemade fermented vegetables, knowing they are safe and delicious.

Fermenting a vegetable for only 2–3 days is not safe!

Recognize and Prevent Molds and Kahm Yeasts

Distinguishing between mold and Kahm yeast is crucial in fermentation to ensure safety and quality. Though they might seem similar, molds and Kahm yeast have distinct features:

Identifying Molds

Appearance: Molds can show up as green, black, red, or pink layers with a fuzzy or fluffy texture and might appear both on and beneath the brine's surface.

Identifying Kahm Yeast

Appearance: Kahm yeast presents as a thin white layer or film on the brine's surface, smooth or slightly rough but not hairy, and only forms on the surface.

Key Differences

Molds typically suggest that the ferment is unsafe and should be discarded, while Kahm yeast is generally harmless and doesn't mean the ferment is spoiled.

Prevention Strategies

Complete submergence: Make sure that the vegetables are completely submerged and that the jar is either hermetically sealed or equipped with a compensating system to limit oxygen exposure.

Correct salt use: Use an appropriate amount of salt, as salt inhibits the growth of yeasts and undesirable microorganisms.

Cutting food: Cut foods into small pieces for more effective and rapid fermentation.

Quality of vegetables: Choose fresh, high-quality vegetables to reduce the risk of yeast and mold development.

Cleanliness of equipment: Keep equipment clean and sanitized to prevent the growth of unwanted microorganisms.

Control temperature: Keep fermentation at controlled temperatures to avoid promoting unwanted growth.

Manage pH levels: Adjust the pH with natural acids (such as lemon juice) without excessively altering the flavor of your ferment.

By following these precautions, you will significantly reduce the occurrence of Kahm yeasts and molds during fermentation."

Quick Guide on Mold and Kahm Yeast in Fermented Foods

Finding mold or Kahm yeast on your ferment isn't a disaster. Here's a straightforward approach to deal with these issues:

- **Mold:** If you're experienced, you might be able to remove the moldy parts and use the rest. If you're new to fermenting, it's safer to throw away the whole batch to avoid any health risks.
- **Kahm yeast:** Simply scrape off the Kahm yeast from the top, close the jar again, and continue the fermentation. If you're not sure, it's best to err on the side of caution and start a new batch. If you decide to go on after removing Kahm yeast, eat the ferment quickly to prevent further problems.

Always aim to prevent mold and yeast before they start. Preventing these issues is much easier and safer than trying to fix them once they've appeared.

CHAPTER 9
PICKLING RECIPES

Vegetables

1. DILLED PICKLED BEANS

INGREDIENTS:

» 2 lb fresh, tender green or yellow beans (5 inches long)
» 4 to 8 heads fresh dill
» ¼ cup canning or pickling salt
» 4 garlic cloves (optional)
» ½ tsp hot red pepper flakes (optional)
» 2 cups white vinegar (5% acidity)
» 2 cups water

Yield: 8 pints

INSTRUCTIONS:

1. Start by washing the beans and trimming off the ends. Cut them into 4-inch lengths.
2. Take each sterile pint jar and add 1 to 2 heads of dill and, if desired, 1 garlic clove.
3. Stand the whole beans upright in the jars, ensuring there's a 1/2-inch space from the top. If needed, trim the beans to fit properly.
4. In a pot, combine the canning or pickling salt, white vinegar, water, and hot red pepper flakes (if using). Boil the mixture.
5. Pour the hot solution over the beans in the jars, leaving a 1/2-inch headspace at the top.
6. Adjust the lids of the jars, follow the processing water bath canning and the recommendations outlined (see notes)
7. Allow to cool for 12–24 hours and check the seals.
8. Shake the jars to disperse the spices before use.

WATER BATH CANNING ALTITUDE ADJUSTMENT CHART AND PROCESS TIME				
Style of Pack	Jar Size	0-1000 Ft	1001-6000 Ft	Above 6,000 Ft
Raw	Pints	5 min	10 min	15 min

2. GREEN TOMATO DILL PICKLES

INGREDIENTS:

» Approximately 2 ½–3 lb small, firm green tomatoes
» 3 small to medium sweet green peppers, seeded and cut
» 3 garlic cloves
» 3 celery stalks, cut into 2-inch lengths
» 1-quart water
» ½ cup pickling salt
» 2 cups distilled white vinegar (5%)
» Fresh dill, to taste

Yield: About 3 quarts' jars

INSTRUCTIONS:

1. Prepare the vegetables: Remove stems and cores from the green peppers, quarter them, and discard seeds. Wash and drain all vegetables. Place washed tomatoes into hot jars. Add to each jar: 1 garlic clove, a stalk of celery, and 2 quarters of green pepper.
2. Make the brine: Mix water, vinegar, and salt in a pot. Add fresh dill. Bring the mixture to a boil and continue boiling for 5 minutes.
3. Jar the pickles: Carefully pour the hot brine over the vegetables in the jars, ensuring there is a ½ inch headspace at the top. Release any trapped air bubbles and adjust the headspace as necessary. Clean the rims of the jars with a damp paper towel. Securely place and adjust the two-piece metal canning lids.
4. Process in a boiling water canner according to the manufacturer's instructions.
5. Maturation: Wait 4 to 6 weeks before consuming to allow the flavors to develop.

Note: It's important to read guidelines on using boiling water canners and the principles of home canning, especially if you're new to the process. This will ensure safety and quality in your canning projects.

WATER BATH CANNING ALTITUDE ADJUSTMENT CHART AND PROCESS TIME				
Style of Pack	Jar Size	0-1000 Ft	1001-6000 Ft	Above 6,000 Ft

Water Bath Canning Altitude Adjustment Chart and Process Time				
Raw	Quarts	15 min	20 min	25 min

3. BEETROOT PICKLES

INGREDIENTS:

- » 3 ½ lb beets, with a diameter of 2 to 2-½ inches
- » 1 tsp canning or pickling salt
- » 2 cups vinegar (5% acidity)
- » 1 cup water
- » 1 cup sugar
- » 6 whole cloves
- » 1 cinnamon sticks
- » 2 to 3 onions (optional), with a diameter of 2 to 2-½ inches

Yield: About 4 pints

INSTRUCTIONS:

1. Trim the tops of the beets, leaving about 1 inch of stem and roots to prevent color bleeding. Thoroughly wash the beets and sort them by size.
2. Cook the similar-sized beets in boiling water until tender, which takes approximately 25 to 30 minutes. Drain and discard the liquid. Allow the beets to cool.
3. Remove the roots and stems from the beets, and peel off the skins. Slice the beets into ¼-inch slices. If desired, peel and thinly slice the onions.
4. In a pot, combine the vinegar, salt, sugar, and fresh water. Place the cinnamon sticks and whole cloves in a cheesecloth bag and add it to the vinegar mixture. Bring the mixture to a boil.
5. Add the sliced beets and onions to the pot and simmer for 5 minutes. Remove the spice bag.
6. Fill jars with the cooked beets and onions, and pour the hot vinegar solution over the beets, maintaining a 1/2-inch headspace.
7. Adjust the lids of the jars and process them according to the table's guidelines.

Water Bath Canning Altitude Adjustment Chart and Process Time					
Style of Pack	Jar Size	0-1000 Ft	1001-3000 Ft	3,001-6,000Ft	Above 6,000 Ft
Hot	Quarts/Pint	30 min	35	40	45

4. CARROT PICKLES

INGREDIENTS:

- » 1 ½ lb peeled carrots
- » ½ cup water
- » 2 ½ cups white distilled vinegar (5%)

- » 1 tsp canning salt
- » 4 tsp mustard seed
- » 2 tsp celery seed
- » 1 cup sugar

Yield: About 2-pint jars

INSTRUCTIONS:

1. Sterilize and keep pint canning jars hot until they are used. Prepare the lids and bands as per the manufacturer's instructions.
2. Thoroughly wash, peel, and then rewash the carrots. Slice them into rounds about ½-inch thick.
3. Combine the vinegar, water, sugar, and canning salt in a large pot. Bring to a gentle boil for 3 minutes. Add the carrots, return to a boil, then reduce to a simmer, cooking until the carrots are half-done (about 10 minutes).
4. Place 2 tsp of mustard seed and 1 tsp of celery seed in each hot pint jar.
5. Pack the hot jars with the hot carrot slices, leaving a 1-inch headspace. Pour the hot pickling liquid over the carrots, leaving a ½-inch headspace. Remove any air bubbles and adjust the headspace as needed. Wipe the jar rims with a clean, damp paper towel and secure the two-piece metal canning lids.
6. Process the jars in a boiling water canner as per the recommended times in your canning guide. Allow the jars to cool undisturbed for 12 to 24 hours and then check for proper sealing.
7. Let the pickled carrots sit in the jars for 3 to 5 days before eating for the flavors to develop fully.

WATER BATH CANNING ALTITUDE ADJUSTMENT CHART AND PROCESS TIME				
Style of Pack	Jar Size	0-1000 Ft	1001-6000 Ft	Above 6,000 Ft
Hot	Pints	15 min	20	25

5. BANANA PEPPER RINGS PICKLES

INGREDIENTS:

- » 3 ½–4 ½ lb yellow (banana) peppers
- » 2 cups water
- » 7 ½ tsp canning salt

- » 6 tbsp mustard seed
- » 7 cups cider vinegar (5%)
- » 3 tbsp celery seed

Yield: About 6-pint jars

INSTRUCTIONS:

1. Sterilize and keep 6-pint canning jars hot until use. Follow the manufacturer's instructions for preparing lids and bands.
2. Clean the peppers thoroughly, remove the stem ends, and cut them into ¼-inch thick rings. In a 6-quart Dutch oven or saucepan, mix the cider vinegar, water, and salt. Bring this mixture to a boil.
3. Add ½ tbsp celery seed and 1 tbsp mustard seed to the bottom of each sterilized pint jar. Then, pack the jars with the pepper rings.
4. Pour the boiling pickling liquid over the pepper rings in each jar, ensuring a ½-inch headspace. Release any trapped air bubbles and readjust the headspace as needed. Clean the jar rims with a damp, clean paper towel, and then apply the two-piece metal canning lids.
5. Process the jars in a boiling water canner according to the times specified in your canning guide. After processing, allow the jars to cool undisturbed for 12 to 24 hours, then check the seals.
6. Before using, shake the jar to evenly distribute the spices.

WATER BATH CANNING ALTITUDE ADJUSTMENT CHART AND PROCESS TIME				
Style of Pack	Jar Size	0-1000 Ft	1001-6000 Ft	Above 6,000 Ft

WATER BATH CANNING ALTITUDE ADJUSTMENT CHART AND PROCESS TIME				
Raw	Pints	10 min	15	20

6. DILLED OKRA PICKLES

INGREDIENTS:

- » 3 ½ lb small okra pods
- » 1/3 cup canning or pickling salt
- » 3 small hot peppers

- » 4 to 5 garlic cloves
- » 3 cups water
- » 3 cups vinegar (5%)
- » 2 tsp dill seed

Yield: 4 to 5 pints

INSTRUCTIONS:

1. Begin by washing and trimming the okra pods. Pack the jars tightly with whole okra, ensuring a ½-inch headspace at the top.
2. Place one garlic clove in each jar.
3. In a large saucepan, combine the pickling salt, hot peppers, dill seed, water, and vinegar. Bring this mixture to a boil.
4. Pour the boiling pickling solution over the okra in each jar, again leaving a ½-inch headspace.
5. Adjust the jar lids and process as per the recommendations in the table's guidelines.

Note: It's crucial to read guidelines on using boiling water canners, especially if you are new to canning. For a comprehensive understanding, also read about the Principles of Home Canning. This ensures safe and effective preservation.

WATER BATH CANNING ALTITUDE ADJUSTMENT CHART AND PROCESS TIME				
Style of Pack	Jar Size	0-1000 Ft	1001-6000 Ft	Above 6,000 Ft
Raw	Pints	10 min	15	20

7. MARINATED MUSHROOMS

INGREDIENTS:

- » 3 ½ lb small whole mushrooms
- » ½ tbsp canning or pickling salt
- » ¼ cup finely chopped onions
- » ¼ cup bottled lemon juice
- » 1 ¼ cups white vinegar (5%)

- » 1 cup olive or salad oil
- » 2 tbsp diced pimento
- » ½ tbsp dried basil leaves
- » ½ tbsp oregano leaves
- » 12–13 black peppercorns
- » 1 garlic clove, cut into quarters

Yield: About 2–3 pints

INSTRUCTIONS:

1. Choose fresh, unopened mushrooms with caps smaller than 1-¼ inches in diameter. Clean them thoroughly. Trim the stems, leaving about ¼ inch attached to the cap.
2. Combine the mushrooms with lemon juice and enough water to cover them. Bring this to a boil, then simmer for 5 minutes. After simmering, drain the mushrooms.
3. In a saucepan, mix the olive oil, vinegar, oregano, basil, and salt. Add the chopped onions and pimento to this mixture and bring it to a boil.
4. Place a quarter of a garlic clove and 4–6 peppercorns into each Pint jar.
5. Fill the jars with the mushrooms and the hot oil/vinegar mixture, ensuring a 1/2-inch headspace at the top of each jar.
6. Adjust the lids of the jars and process them according to the table's guidelines.

WATER BATH CANNING ALTITUDE ADJUSTMENT CHART AND PROCESS TIME					
Style of Pack	Jar Size	0-1000 Ft	1001-3000 Ft	3,001-6,000Ft	Above 6,000 Ft
Hot	Pints	20 min	25	30	35

8. BREAD AND BUTTER ZUCCHINI PICKLES

INGREDIENTS:

» 8 cups fresh zucchini, sliced
» ¼ cup canning or pickling salt
» 2 cups onions, thinly sliced
» 1 cup sugar

» 2 cups white vinegar (5%)
» 1 tbsp celery seed
» 1 tsp ground turmeric
» 2 tbsp mustard seed

Yield: About 4 to 5 pints

INSTRUCTIONS:

1. Mix the zucchini and onion slices with enough water to cover them by an inch, then stir in the salt. Leave this to stand for 2 hours before draining thoroughly.
2. In a large pot, combine the vinegar, sugar, mustard seed, celery seed, and ground turmeric. Bring this mixture to a boil.
3. Add the drained zucchini and onions to the boiling mixture. Let it simmer for 5 minutes.
4. Pack the hot zucchini and onion mixture into jars, along with the pickling solution, ensuring there's a ½-inch headspace at the top.
5. Secure the lids on the jars and process them according to the guidelines provided in the table's guidelines, or you can opt for a low-temperature pasteurization treatment.

WATER BATH CANNING ALTITUDE ADJUSTMENT CHART AND PROCESS TIME				
Style of Pack	Jar Size	0-1000 Ft	1001-6000 Ft	Above 6,000 Ft
Hot	Pints	10 min	15	20

Low-Temperature Pasteurization Treatment:

1. Fill the canner halfway with warm water (between 120° and 140°F).
2. Place the jars in the canner, then add more hot water until it's 1 inch above the jars.
3. Heat the water to maintain a temperature between 180° and 185°F for 30 minutes. Use a candy or jelly thermometer to ensure the water stays at least 180°F throughout the 30 minutes.
4. Be careful not to exceed 185°F to avoid over-softening the pickles

Note: Only use this method when the recipe specifically recommends it. This technique helps preserve the texture of the pickles but requires careful temperature management to prevent spoilage.

9. HORSERADISH PICKLES SAUCE

INGREDIENTS:

- » 4 cups freshly grated horseradish
- » 1 tsp canning or pickling salt
- » 2 cups raw apple vinegar (5%)
- » ½ tsp powdered ascorbic acid

Yield: About 2 pints

INSTRUCTIONS:

1. Horseradish loses its intensity quickly, usually within 1 to 2 months, even under refrigeration, so it's best to prepare small batches. Start by thoroughly cleaning the horseradish roots and removing the brown outer skin.
2. You can grate the peeled horseradish using a food processor, or alternatively, chop it into small cubes and process them through a food grinder.
3. Mix the freshly grated or ground horseradish with the vinegar, canning salt, and powdered ascorbic acid.
4. Transfer this mixture into sterilized jars, making sure to leave a ¼-inch headspace at the top of each jar.
5. Securely seal the jars and refrigerate them.

Note:

- Remember that fresh horseradish must be used promptly as it loses its pungency over time, even if it is refrigerated, so it is best to prepare small lots.
- Adding ascorbic acid or lemon juice is optional and serves to minimize browning.
- The use of a sweetener is also optional and is intended to enhance and balance the flavor.

10. HOT PEPPERS PICKLES

INGREDIENTS:

- » 2 lb hot long green, yellow, or red peppers
- » 1 ½ lb mixed sweet green and red peppers
- » 2 ½ cups vinegar (5%)

- » ½ cup water
- » 2 tsp canning or pickling salt
- » 1 tbsp sugar
- » 1 garlic clove

Yield: About 4–5 pints

INSTRUCTIONS:

1. Thoroughly wash the peppers. For small peppers, make 2 to 4 slits in each; quarter the larger peppers. Blanch them in boiling water or use a blistering method for peeling. To blister peppers, either use an oven or broiler at 400ºF for 6–8 minutes or place them on a heavy wire mesh over a hot burner until their skins blister. Once blistered, cool the peppers and peel off the skin. Flatten the small peppers.
2. Sterilize your jars, keeping them hot until use. Prepare lids and bands according to the manufacturer's instructions.
3. In a pot, combine the vinegar, water, canning salt, sugar, and garlic. Bring this mixture to a boil, then simmer for 10 minutes. Remove the garlic afterward.
4. Pack the peppers into the jars, leaving a 1/2-inch headspace at the top. Pour the hot pickling solution over the peppers, maintaining the same headspace.
5. Adjust the jar lids and process in a boiling water canner as per the instructions provided in the table's guidelines.

Note: When handling hot peppers, it's advised to wear rubber gloves to avoid skin irritation, or wash your hands thoroughly with soap and water before touching your face or sensitive areas.

WATER BATH CANNING ALTITUDE ADJUSTMENT CHART AND PROCESS TIME				
Style of Pack	Jar Size	0-1000 Ft	1001-6000 Ft	Above 6,000 Ft
Raw	Pints	10 min	15	20

11. ASPARAGUS PICKLES

INGREDIENTS:

- » 5 lb asparagus
- » 2 ¼ cups water
- » 2 ¼ cups white vinegar (5%)

- » 3 large garlic cloves
- » 3 small hot pepper
- » ¼ cup canning salt
- » 1 ½ tsp dill seed

Yield: About 3–4 pints

INSTRUCTIONS:

1. Clean and heat jars for canning. Follow the specific lid preparation method provided by the lid manufacturer.
2. Thoroughly rinse the asparagus. Trim the ends to ensure the spears are slightly shorter than the jar height, leaving just a bit less than half an inch of space at the top. Peel the garlic cloves and place one in the bottom of each jar. Arrange the asparagus in the jars, with the tips facing up.
3. Create the brine by combining water, vinegar, salt, dill seed, and optional hot peppers in a large pot. Heat until it reaches a boil.
4. If using hot peppers, add one to each jar atop the asparagus. Pour the hot brine over the asparagus in each jar, maintaining a half-inch space from the top.
5. Eliminate air pockets and make sure the headspace is correctly adjusted. Clean the rim of each jar with a moist, clean towel, then fix the two-piece metal lids in place.
6. Process the jars in a water bath canner as outlined in your canning instructions. After processing, let the jars cool without moving them for 12 to 24 hours, then check the seals.
7. For the best flavor development, let the pickled asparagus rest in the jars for 3 to 5 days before consuming.
8. Adjust the lids of the jars and process them according to the table's guidelines.

WATER BATH CANNING ALTITUDE ADJUSTMENT CHART AND PROCESS TIME				
Style of Pack	Jar Size	0-1000 Ft	1001-6000 Ft	Above 6,000 Ft
Raw	Pints	10 min	15	20

12. BRUSSELS SPROUTS PICKLES WITH TURMERIC

INGREDIENTS:

- » 6 cups small Brussels sprouts
- » ½ cup sweet red peppers
- » 1 cup sugar
- » 1 cup onions

- » 2 cups white vinegar (5%)
- » 1 tbsp mustard seed
- » ½ tsp hot red pepper flakes
- » ½ tbsp celery seed
- » ½ tsp turmeric

Yield: About 2–3 pints

INSTRUCTIONS:

1. Prepare the Brussels sprouts by washing them, and removing the stems and any damaged outer leaves. Boil them in salted water (2 tsp canning salt per gallon of water) for 4 minutes. After boiling, drain and let them cool.
2. In a large saucepan, mix the vinegar, sugar, thinly sliced onions, diced red peppers, mustard seed, celery seed, turmeric, and red pepper flakes. Bring this mixture to a boil, then let it simmer for 5 minutes.
3. Evenly distribute the onions and red peppers into the jars. Then pack the jars with Brussels sprouts and cover them with the hot pickling solution, leaving a half-inch of space at the top of each jar.

Note: Always ensure to follow safe canning practices and consult the latest guidelines for boiling water canning. This recipe is great for preserving Brussels sprouts and adds a flavorful twist with the pickling spices.

WATER BATH CANNING ALTITUDE ADJUSTMENT CHART AND PROCESS TIME				
Style of Pack	Jar Size	0-1000 Ft	1001-6000 Ft	Above 6,000 Ft
Hot	Pints	10 min	15	20

13. CAULIFLOWER PICKLES WITH TURMERIC AND GINGER

INGREDIENTS:

» 6 cups cauliflower florets
» 4 pieces ginger root,
» 6 pieces turmeric root,
» 6 Thai chilies, halved lengthwise (or ½ tsp red pepper flakes)

» 3 cups white vinegar
» 1 ½ cups water
» 4–5 large garlic cloves,
» 1 ½ tbsp pickling or Kosher salt
» 1 cup sugar

Yield: About 3–4 half-pints

INSTRUCTIONS:

1. Cut the cauliflower into bite-sized florets (about 1 ½ inches) and discard the tough stems.
2. Peel and slice the ginger and turmeric into thin matchsticks of 2–3 inches each.
3. Prepare the chilies by removing the stems and slicing them in half lengthwise. Keep the seeds and membranes for extra heat, or slice them into thin strips.
4. In a large saucepan, combine the vinegar, water, peeled and crushed garlic, salt, and sugar. Stir to dissolve the salt and sugar, then bring to a boil. Reduce heat, simmer for 5 minutes, and then turn off the heat. Let the brine cool for about 10 minutes.
5. Add the ginger, turmeric, chilies, and cauliflower to the warm brine. Stir and let it sit for 10 minutes, or until the cauliflower is tender but still firm.
6. Transfer the vegetables to a large glass bowl or a gallon jar with a lid, using a ladle or slotted spoon. Pour enough hot brine over the vegetables to fully submerge them. Discard any excess brine.
7. Refrigerate the pickled vegetables in a covered container for up to 3 weeks. They will be ready to eat in 24–48 hours, but the flavor improves the longer they sit in the brine.

Note:

- The pickling process enhances the cauliflower's taste over two days, and it gets even better with time.
- Include red pepper flakes in the boiling mixture if you're substituting them for Thai chilies. These flakes should remain in the liquid throughout the pickling process.
- Keep in mind that the nutritional values stated account for the entire brine volume. Since not all of it may be used or consumed, the actual carbohydrate and sodium levels will likely be lower.

If you want to keep them longer, you can process them in a bain-marie by consulting the table's guidelines.

WATER BATH CANNING ALTITUDE ADJUSTMENT CHART AND PROCESS TIME				
Style of Pack	Jar Size	0-1000 Ft	1001-6000 Ft	Above 6,000 Ft
Hot	Pints	10 min	15	20

14. SWEET PEPPERS PICKLES

INGREDIENTS:

» 3 ½ lb firm bell peppers
» 1 ½ cups sugar
» 1 ½ cups vinegar (5%)

» 1 ½ cups water
» 4–5 garlic cloves
» 2 ¼ tsp canning or pickling salt

Yield: About 4 ½ pints

INSTRUCTIONS:

1. Clean the peppers, slice them into quarters, and remove the cores, seeds, and any imperfect spots. Then, cut the peppers into strips.
2. In a pot, bring the sugar, vinegar, and water to a boil for 1 minute. Add the pepper strips and return to a boil.
3. For each sterilized half-pint jar, add ¼ garlic clove and 1/8 tsp of salt; double these amounts if you are using pint jars.
4. Pack the jars with the pepper strips and pour the hot vinegar mixture over them, ensuring a 1/2-inch headspace at the top of each jar.
5. Secure the lids on the jars and process them in a boiling water canner as specified in your canning guide or table.

Note: If you're new to canning, it's important to familiarize yourself with using boiling water canners and to understand the principles of home canning to ensure the safety and quality of your pickled peppers.

WATER BATH CANNING ALTITUDE ADJUSTMENT CHART AND PROCESS TIME				
Style of Pack	Jar Size	0-1000 Ft	1001-6000 Ft	Above 6,000 Ft
Hot	Pints	5 min	10	15

15. SWEET GREEN CHERRY TOMATO PICKLES

INGREDIENTS:

»   5 lb green cherry tomatoes (approx. 8 cups sliced)
»   2 cups vinegar (5%)
»   1 cup sliced onions
»   4 tbsp canning or pickling salt
»   1 ½ cups brown sugar
»   **Basic Pickling Spice Mix:**
»   ½ tbsp yellow mustard seeds
»   ½ tbsp whole cloves
»   2 tsp coriander seed
»   ½ tbsp whole allspice
»   ½ tbsp celery seed

Yields: About 4–5 pints.

INSTRUCTIONS:

1. Start by washing and slicing the tomatoes and onions. Place them in a bowl and sprinkle with ¼ cup salt. Let them sit for 4–6 hours, then drain.
2. In a saucepan, heat and stir the sugar into the vinegar until it dissolves completely.
3. Prepare a spice bag by binding together the mustard seeds, allspice, celery seeds, coriander seeds, and cloves. Add the spice bag to the vinegar mixture along with the tomatoes and onions. If necessary, add a small amount of water to ensure the pieces are covered.
4. Bring the mixture to a boil and let it simmer for 30 minutes, stirring occasionally to prevent burning. The tomatoes should become tender and transparent when well cooked.
5. Remove the spice bag from the mixture. Fill jars with cooked tomatoes and onions and cover with hot pickling solution, leaving ½ inch headspace.
6. Adjust the lids on the jars and process them according to the recommendations given in the table's guidelines.

WATER BATH CANNING ALTITUDE ADJUSTMENT CHART AND PROCESS TIME				
Style of Pack	Jar Size	0-1000 Ft	1001-6000 Ft	Above 6,000 Ft
Hot	Pints	10 min	15	20

Fresh-pack or Quick-process Recipes

16. PICKLED MUSTARD CUCUMBER

INGREDIENTS:

»   2 lb cucumbers (approx. 4 medium-sized)
»   ½ lb (approx. 2 small onions)
»   2 ½ cups water
»   2 ½ cups vinegar (5% acidity)

»   2 tbsp canning or pickling salt
»   2 ½ cups rice syrup (or Sucralose Splenda)
»   ½ cup fresh dill
»   4 tbsp yellow mustard seeds

Yields. About 6–7 pints.

INSTRUCTIONS:

1. Peel the cucumber, halve it, remove the seeds, and cut it into 1 cm cubes. Peel and cut the onions into quarters.
2. Place the cucumber cubes and quartered onions in a pot. Add the water, vinegar, rice syrup, mustard seeds and salt.
3. Bring to a boil, stirring occasionally.
4. Reduce heat and let simmer for 2 minutes.
5. Coarsely chop 1/3 ounce of dill. Transfer the contents of the pot to a sterile jar, add the chopped dill, and seal the jar tightly.
6. Allow to marinate in the refrigerator for at least 2 weeks.

Note: It is important to follow the instructions of any recipe carefully, especially if it involves cooking or handling hot ingredients.

17. QUICK DILL PICKLES

INGREDIENTS:

»   4 lb pickling cucumbers, 3 to 5 inches long
»   6 tbsp pickling salt
»   1-gallon water (for brine)
»   ¼ cup canning and pickling salt
»   2 tbsp sugar

»   ¾ quart vinegar (5%)
»   1-quart water (for pickling liquid)
»   1 tbsp mixed pickling spice (whole)
»   1 ½ tbsp mustard seed (½ tbsp per pint jar)
»   6 heads fresh dill (¾ head per pint jar) or 1 tbsp dill seed (¾ tbsp per pint jar)

Yield: Makes about 3–5 pints

INSTRUCTIONS:

1. Wash the cucumbers, keeping a ¼-inch stem and slicing off 1/16-inch from the blossom end.
2. Create a brine by dissolving 6 tbsp of salt in 1 gallon of water. Soak the cucumbers in this brine for 12 hours before draining.
3. In another pot, mix the vinegar, ¼ cup of salt, sugar, and 1 quart of water. Include the pickling spices tied in a cloth. Boil the mixture, then remove the spice bag.
4. Fill sterilized jars with cucumbers. Add ½ tbsp of mustard seed and about ¾ head of fresh dill to each pint jar.
5. Pour the boiling pickling liquid over the cucumbers, leaving a ½ inch headspace. Ensure cucumbers are fully submerged. Use a spatula to remove air bubbles.
6. Secure the jar lids and process in a boiling water canner for 10 minutes for pints or 15 minutes for quarts.

18. CLASSIC BREAD AND BUTTER PICKLES

INGREDIENTS:

» 3 lb pickling cucumbers, 4 to 5 inches long, or slender zucchini
» 1 ½ lb onions, peeled and thinly sliced
» Crushed or cubed ice
» ¼ cup canning and pickling salt
» **Pickling Solution:**
» 2 cups vinegar (5%)
» 2 cups sugar
» 1 ½ tsp ground mustard
» 2 tsp celery seed
» 1 tbsp mustard seed

Yield: It makes about 3 ½ to 4 pints.

INSTRUCTIONS:

1. Wash the cucumbers or zucchini carefully. Trim and discard 1/16 inch from the blossom end. Slice them into 3/16-inch-thick slices. Mix the cucumbers or zucchini and sliced onions in a large bowl. Sprinkle with salt and cover with 2 inches of ice. Refrigerate for 3–5 hours, replenishing ice as necessary. Then, drain the mixture well.
2. For the pickling solution, combine the sugar, vinegar, and spices in a large pot. Bring it to a boil and continue boiling for 10 minutes. Add the drained cucumbers or squash and onions, and slowly bring back to a boil.
3. Pack the pickle slices and pickling liquid into clean, hot pint jars, leaving 1/2-inch of headspace. Use a spatula to remove air bubbles. Wipe the jar rims with a clean, damp cloth.

Close the jars firmly with the lids and process them in the boiling water pot according to the table's guidelines.

Note: For best flavor, let the jars sit for 4 to 5 weeks after processing and cooling before consuming. This recipe is perfect for smaller batches of homemade bread and butter pickles.

WATER BATH CANNING ALTITUDE ADJUSTMENT CHART AND PROCESS TIME				
Style of Pack	Jar Size	0-1000 Ft	1001-6000 Ft	Above 6,000 Ft
Hot	Pints	10 min	15	20

19. QUICK SWEET PICKLED CUCUMBERS

INGREDIENTS:

» 4 lb pickling cucumbers, 3 to 4 inches in length
» 1/3 cup canning and pickling salt
» Crushed or cubed ice
» **Pickling Solution:**

Yield: Makes 4 to 5 pints.

» 2 cups sugar
» 1 ¾ cups vinegar (5%)
» 1 tbsp mustard seed
» 1 tbsp celery seed
» 1 ½ tbsp whole allspice

INSTRUCTIONS:

1. Wash the cucumbers gently. Remove 1/16 inch from the blossom end and discard it, but keep a 1/4-inch stem. Slice cucumbers or cut into strips.
2. In a bowl, mix cucumbers with 1/6 cup salt and cover with 2 inches of ice. Refrigerate for 3 to 4 hours, replenishing ice as necessary. Then, drain the cucumbers well.
3. In a 3-quart kettle, prepare the pickling solution by boiling together sugar, vinegar, celery seed, allspice, and mustard seed.
4. For the Hot Pack method: Heat cucumbers in pickling solution until boiling, then pack into jars with a 1/2-inch headspace. Cover cucumbers with the boiling solution, maintaining headspace. Remove air bubbles, wipe jar rims, seal with lids, and process in a water canner for 5 minutes for pint jars.
5. Or, for the Raw Pack method: Pack jars with drained cucumbers, and cover with boiling pickling solution, leaving 1/2-inch headspace. Remove air bubbles and wipe jar rims. Seal jars with pretreated lids.

   • Process in a boiling water canner: 10 minutes for pints, 15 minutes for quarts, or use low-temperature pasteurization.

Note: After processing and cooling, let jars sit for 4 to 5 weeks for flavors to fully develop. This recipe is perfect for smaller batches and offers a sweet, spiced cucumber pickle.

Sterilizing jars

If the recipe calls for a **short processing time**— less than 10 minutes—wash jars in warm, soapy water, and rinse. **Sterilize jars by boiling for 10 minutes.** Keep hot until filled. **Recipes for refrigerator pickles are not heat-processed and jars must also be sterilized by boiling for 10 minutes before filling.**

---

20. LOW SODIUM DILL PICKLE SLICES

INGREDIENTS:

» 2 lb pickling cucumbers, 3 to 5 inches long
» 3 cups sugar
» 1 tbsp canning and pickling salt
» 3 cups vinegar (5%)

» ¾ tsp mustard seed
» ¾ tsp celery seed
» 3–4 fresh dill heads
» 1 large onion, thinly sliced

Yield: 4 pints.

INSTRUCTIONS:

1. Wash the cucumbers thoroughly. Trim off and discard 1/16 inch from the blossom end. Slice the cucumbers into ¼-inch pieces.
2. In a medium saucepan, mix the vinegar, sugar, salt, celery seeds, and mustard seeds. Bring this mixture to a boil.
3. Arrange 2 onion slices and ½ dill head at the bottom of each hot pint jar. Pack the jars with cucumber slices, leaving 1/2-inch headspace. Place another onion slice and ½ dill head on top. Pour the boiling pickling solution over the cucumbers, ensuring a ¼-inch headspace. Use a spatula to remove air bubbles and clean the jar rims with a damp cloth.
4. Seal the jars with pretreated lids and adjust them properly.
5. Process the jars in a boiling water canner for **15 minutes for pints** Altitudes **1.000 ft.** and **20 minutes for 1.001–6.000 ft.** Altitudes.

21. SUGAR-FREE SWEET PICKLE SLICES

INGREDIENTS:

» 5 lb pickling cucumbers, sliced
» Boiling water (enough to cover the cucumber slices)
» 6 cups cider vinegar (5%)
» 4 ½ cups Sucralose Splenda (a sugar substitute)
» 1 ½ tbsp canning salt

» 1 ½ cups water
» 1 ½ tbsp mustard seed
» 1 ½ tbsp whole allspice
» 1 ½ tbsp celery seed
» 5 one-inch cinnamon sticks (optional)

Yield: 4 or 5 pints

INSTRUCTIONS:

1. Wash the cucumber slice off and discard 1/16 inch from the blossom ends. Cut the cucumbers into ¼-inch-thick slices.
2. Pour boiling water over the cucumber slices and let them stand for 5 to 10 minutes. Then, drain the hot water and cool the slices by running cold water over them or changing the water frequently. Drain well after cooling.
3. In a large stockpot (around 15 quarts), combine 6 cups of vinegar, 1 ½ cups of water, 4½ cups of Sucralose Splenda, and all the spices. Bring this to a boil. Then, add the drained cucumber slices and bring back to a boil.
4. Optionally, place a cinnamon stick in each jar. Use a slotted spoon to fill the hot cucumber slices into clean, hot pint jars, leaving a 1/2-inch headspace. Pour the boiling pickling brine over the slices, also leaving a 1/2-inch headspace. Remove any air bubbles, wipe the jar rims, and adjust the lids.
5. Process the jars in a boiling water canner for **10 minutes for pints** Altitudes **1.000 ft.** and **15 minutes for 1.001–6.000 ft.** Altitudes.

22. LOW-SODIUM SWEET PICKLE SLICES

INGREDIENTS:

» 6 lb pickling cucumbers (3-inch)
» **Canning syrup:**
» 2 ½ cups distilled white vinegar (5%)
» 4 ½ cups sugar
» 3 tsp celery seed

» 1 ½ tbsp whole allspice
» **Brining solution:**
» 1 ½ quart distilled white vinegar (5%)
» 1 ½ tbsp pickling or canning salt
» 8 tbsp sugar
» 1 ½ tbsp mustard seed

Yield: About 6–7 pints.

INSTRUCTIONS:

1. Wash the cucumbers and remove 1/16 inch from the blossom end. Slice cucumbers into ¼-inch-thick slices.
2. For the canning syrup, mix vinegar, sugar, celery seed, and allspice in a saucepan. Bring it to a boil, then keep it hot until used.
3. In a larger kettle, combine the ingredients for the brining solution. Add cucumber slices, cover, and simmer until they change color from bright to dull green (about 5 to 7 minutes). Drain the slices.
4. Pack the hot pint jars with cucumber slices. Pour the hot canning syrup over the slices, leaving a 1/2-inch headspace. Remove any air bubbles, wipe the jar rims, and adjust the lids.

This sweet pickle recipe has a lower sodium content, ideal for those looking for a healthier pickle option.

Process the jars in a boiling water canner for **10 minutes for pints** Altitudes **1.000 ft.** and **15 minutes for 1.001–6.000 ft.** Altitudes.

23. QUICK SWEET RADISH PICKLES

INGREDIENTS:

»   2 bunches radish (about 1 lb), without stem and roots and cut into 1/8-inch slices
»   ½ cup water
»   1 cup sugar
»   2 tsp Salt for Pickling
»   1 cup white or apple cider vinegar (5% acidity)
»   2 tsp mustard seeds
»   2 bay leafs
»   1 tsp ground black pepper
»   1 tsp dried crushed red pepper (optional)
»   1 tsp coriander seed

Yield: About 2 pints.

INSTRUCTIONS:

1.   Place the sliced radishes in a sterilized 1-pint jar.
2.   In a small stainless steel or enameled saucepan, bring the vinegar, sugar, water, Salt, mustard seeds, black pepper, bay leaf, and crushed red pepper (if using) to a boil.
3.   pour the hot pickling liquid over the radishes in the jar.
4.   Clean the edge of the jar to ensure a clean seal. Place the lid on the jar and tighten it with your fingertips.
5.   Allow the jar to cool on a wire rack for approximately 1 hour.
6.   Store the jar in the refrigerator for at least 6 hours before serving.

Since these are quick pickles, remember to always keep them in the fridge. They are ideally consumed within 1 to 2 weeks for the best taste.

24. CUCUMBER AND ONIONS REFRESHING PICKLES

INGREDIENTS:

- » 4 cups cucumbers, thinly sliced
- » ½ cup onion, peeled and sliced (1 medium onion)
- » You can also replace the onion with an equal amount of other vegetables such as cauliflower, peppers, or carrots, as needed.

Pickling solution:

Yield: About 2 pints

- » 1 cup sugar
- » 2 ½ tbsp pickling salt
- » 2 cups vinegar (5%)
- » ½ tsp celery seed
- » ½ tsp mustard seed
- » ½ tsp turmeric seed.

INSTRUCTIONS:

1. In a bowl, mix the pickling solution ingredients until the sugar is dissolved. You can heat the mixture to dissolve the sugar more quickly.
2. Wash and prepare the vegetables. Cut off the flower ends of the cucumbers and discard them.
3. Fill hot sterilized half-liter or quart jars with the thinly sliced cucumbers and other chosen vegetables.
4. Pour the hot pickling solution over the vegetables in the jars, making sure they are completely covered. Close the jars with clean lids.
5. Label and date the jars, then store them in the refrigerator at 40°F or colder for up to 2 weeks.

25. JAPANESE STYLE PICKLED RED CABBAGE

INGREDIENTS:

- » 4 cups red cabbage
- » 2 ½ quart water
- » 2 fresh lemons
- » 2 cups red wine vinegar
- » 1 cup white wine

- » 4 tbsp sugar
- » 4 tsp sea salt (or pickling salt)
- » 2 bay leave
- » 1 tsp mixed peppercorns
- » 1 tsp coriander seeds

Yield: About 2–3 pints

INSTRUCTIONS:

1. Wash the cabbage in cold running water. Cut the cabbage into quarters and discard the outer leaves. Cut away the hard central core and shred the remaining cabbage finely.
2. In a saucepan, combine all ingredients; vinegar, bay leaf, pepper, lemon juice, sugar, and salt; heat over medium heat. Once it boils, turn off the heat and set it aside.
3. Cook the cabbage; In a medium pan, bring the water to a boil over medium heat. Add the thinly sliced cabbage and blanch until it turns bluish. Drain the cabbage well.
4. Place the cooked cabbage in sterilized jars, add the brine liquid over the cabbage, and let it be completely submerged. Let cool and refrigerate for at least 24 hours before serving.

You can store it in the refrigerator for up to 1 month.

Delicious pickled red cabbage is an easy and quick recipe, perfect for salads, tacos, hamburgers, sandwiches, rice accompaniments, and much more.

Recipe Notes: The red cabbage was boiled and then drained, which intensified its color, making it more vibrant. This method of preparation facilitates the rapid absorption of the pickling sauce into the cabbage, leading to a remarkable transformation of the cabbage into a striking pink hue!

Red wine vinegar: I love the flavor of red wine vinegar and its combination with fresh lemon juice for this recipe. I also found that the color becomes more striking with it.

Any type of vinegar can work so try your favorite from your kitchen cupboard. Note that rice vinegar is milder than standard white vinegar. Apple cider vinegar works well too.

White wine: The pickling sauce is brought to the boil so that the alcohol is released. I've found that with white wine, pickled cabbage becomes more flavorful.

26. FENNEL AND ORANGE PICKLES

INGREDIENTS:

» 4 ½ fennel bulb
» 12–15 fennel leaves (reserved from the fennel bulb)
» 2 ½ cups cider vinegar (5%)
» 6 bird's-eye chilies or (Thai chilies)
» 1 cup water
» 5 tbsp cane granulated sugar

» 2 ¼ tsp sea salt
» Zest 3 oranges
» Zest 1 lemon
» 2 tsp yellow mustard seeds
» 1 ½ tsp chili flakes
» 1 tsp black peppercorns

Yields: about 4–5 pints.

INSTRUCTIONS:

1. Prepare the fennel bulb by removing the top and bottom, and slicing off the stalks. Save some leaves for later. Finely slice the bulb, either using a mandolin or a sharp knife. Finely chop the chilies, removing seeds if preferred.
2. In a medium stainless-steel pan, combine all other ingredients (excluding the reserved fennel leaves). Include the chopped chilies. Simmer for about 5 minutes until the sugar dissolves and the spices infuse.
3. Take the pan off the heat and allow it to cool slightly.
4. Pack the sliced fennel into warm, sterilized jars, leaving about 1 cm from the top. Tap the jars to remove air bubbles. Top up with the brine if needed.
5. Place a few of the reserved fennel leaves in each jar and seal the jars.
6. The pickle is ready to eat in a few days but can be stored and sealed in a cool, dark place for 3 weeks for marinating. It keeps for up to 4–6 months unopened. Once opened, refrigerate and consume within 4 weeks.

This enhanced recipe is perfect for those who enjoy a natural aniseed flavor from the fennel, balanced with the citrusy zest of oranges.

27. PICKLED RED ONION AND LIME

INGREDIENTS:

» 7–8 medium red onions, peeled and sliced
» 3 cups boiling water
» 3 limes, thinly sliced
» 2 cups distilled vinegar (5%)

» 3 tbsp granulated sugar
» 1 ½ tbsp salt
» 1 ½ tbsp peppercorns
» 1 ½ tbsp dried coriander

Yields: about 3–4 pints.

INSTRUCTIONS:

1. Peel and slice the onions into half-moon shapes, place them in the pot, and cover them with boiling water, making sure they are completely submerged.
2. After soaking for one minute, drain the onions. Store the water in a separate saucepan. Place the drained onions and lime slices in a sterilized jar.
3. In the saucepan with the reserved onion water, add the vinegar, sugar, salt, peppercorns, and dried coriander. Bring this to a boil for 5 minutes, stirring to make sure everything dissolves properly.
4. Allow the boiling mixture to cool for about 10 minutes—don't' pour it boiling into the jar, then add it to the onion and lime mixture in the jar until nearly full.
5. Close the jar and let it cool before storing it in the refrigerator. For the best flavor, let the pickle sit for at least 24 hours before enjoying it.

You can store them in the refrigerator for up to 3 weeks.

This recipe is perfect with meats, salads, or as a topping for a burger, adding a delightful zesty twist.

28. GINGER SPICED CRABAPPLES

INGREDIENTS:

» 2 ½ lb crabapples
» 3 ½ cups sugar
» 3 ½-inch cubes fresh ginger root

» 2 ¼ cups apple cider vinegar (5%)
» 1 ½ cups water
» 2 sticks cinnamon
» 2 tsp whole cloves

Yield: About 4–5 pints

INSTRUCTIONS:

1. Prepare the crabapples by removing any blossom petals and washing them. Leave the stems attached. Use an awl or toothpick to puncture the skin of each apple four times.
2. In a large pot, combine the apple cider vinegar, water, and sugar. Bring the mixture to a boil.
3. Tie the whole cloves, cinnamon sticks, and fresh ginger root in a spice bag or cheesecloth.
4. In batches, blanch about one-third of the crabapples at a time in boiling vinegar and syrup for 2 minutes, using a blancher basket or sieve.
5. Transfer the blanched apples and spice bag into a 1- or 2-gallon clean crock. Pour the hot syrup over the apples, cover the crock, and let it rest overnight.
6. The next day, take out the spice bag and pour the syrup back into a large saucepan. Bring it to a boil.
7. Pack the cooked crabapples into pint jars and fill them with the reheated syrup, leaving a ½-inch space at the top of each jar.
8. Secure the lids on the jars and process them as per the specific canning guidelines provided in your reference table.

WATER BATH CANNING ALTITUDE ADJUSTMENT CHART AND PROCESS TIME					
Style of Pack	Jar Size	0-1000 Ft	1001-3000 Ft	3,001-6,000Ft	Above 6,000 Ft
Hot	Pints	20 min	25	30	35

29. CINNAMON FIG PICKLES

INGREDIENTS:

» 8 cups firm-ripe figs
» 1 ½ cups vinegar
» 1-quart water
» 1 ½ cups sugar (for initial cooking)
» 1 cup sugar (to add later)
» ½ tbsp whole cloves
» 1 stick cinnamon
» ½ tbsp whole allspice

Yield: About 4 pints.

INSTRUCTIONS:

1. Peel the figs. If you prefer them unpeeled, soak them in boiling water until cool, then drain.
2. Dissolve 1 ½ cups of sugar in 1 quart of water over heat. Add the figs and simmer for 30 minutes.
3. Stir in an additional 1 cup of sugar and 1 ½ cups of vinegar.
4. Place the cinnamon, allspice, and cloves in a cheesecloth bag and add it to the fig mixture. Cook until the figs are translucent. Then, cover and refrigerate for 12 to 24 hours.
5. Remove the spice bag. Reheat the figs in their brine until boiling.
6. Pack the hot figs and brine into sterilized jars, leaving a ½-inch headspace. Remove any air bubbles and adjust the headspace as needed. Wipe the jar rims with a damp, clean paper towel and secure the canning lids.

Process the jars in a boiling water canner according to the recommended time provided in the table's guidelines

WATER BATH CANNING ALTITUDE ADJUSTMENT CHART AND PROCESS TIME				
Style of Pack	Jar Size	0-1000 Ft	1001-6000 Ft	Above 6,000 Ft
Hot	Pints	15 min	20	20

30. CINNAMON SPICED CRABAPPLES

INGREDIENTS:

- » 4 cups crabapples with stems
- » 1 ½ cups white vinegar (5%)
- » 3 cups sugar
- » 1 ½ cups water

Yield: About 3 pints

- » **Spice Bag:**
- » ½ tbsp whole cloves
- » ½ tbsp allspice
- » ½ stick cinnamon
- » ½ tsp coriander seeds

INSTRUCTIONS:

1. Select round, uniformly sized crabapples. Remove blossom petals but keep the short stems. Wash and drain them. To prevent the skins from bursting, pierce them with a large sterilized needle.
2. In a pot, mix the vinegar, water, and sugar. Place the spices in a bag and add it to the mixture. Boil until the syrup thickens enough to coat a spoon.
3. Gently add the crabapples to the syrup and reheat slowly to keep the skins from bursting. Simmer until the apples are tender.
4. Place the hot crabapples in hot jars, leaving a ½-inch headspace. Pour the boiling syrup over the apples, ensuring they are fully submerged, and leaving ½-inch space from the top.
5. Release any air bubbles and adjust the headspace as necessary. Wipe the jar rims with a damp, clean paper towel and secure with two-piece metal lids.
6. Process the jars in a boiling water canner according to canning guidelines.

WATER BATH CANNING ALTITUDE ADJUSTMENT CHART AND PROCESS TIME					
Style of Pack	Jar Size	0-1000 Ft	1001-3000 Ft	3,001-6,000Ft	Above 6,000 Ft
Hot	Pints	20 min	25	30	35

31. SWEET PICKLED WATERMELON RIND

INGREDIENTS:

» 9 lb unpared watermelon rind (4 ½ quarts)
» 4 ½ cups water
» 3 quarts ice cubes
» 4 ½ cups white vinegar (5%)
» 4 ½ quarts water
» 1 ½ lemon, thinly sliced and stripped of seeds

» 1 cup + 2 tbsp pickling salt
» 13 cups sugar
» **Spice bag:**
» 1 ½ tbsp whole cloves
» 9 cinnamon sticks (1-inch pieces)
» 7 stars anise

Yield: about 6 to 7 pints

INSTRUCTIONS:

1. **Prepare Watermelon Rind:** Trim pink flesh and outer green skin from the rind. Cut into 1-inch squares or desired shapes. Mix brine with salt and 4 ½ quarts cold water, add ice cubes. Soak rind for 3–4 hours.
2. **Cook Rind:** Drain rind, rinse in cold water, then cover with fresh cold water. Cook until fork-tender, about 10 minutes. Drain.
3. **Prepare Syrup:** Mix sugar, vinegar, 4 ½ cups water, and spices (enclosed in a clean, thin, white cloth). Boil for 5 minutes, then pour over the watermelon rind and add lemon slices. Refrigerate overnight.
4. **Cook Pickles:** Heat watermelon in syrup to boiling. Cook slowly for 1 hour.
5. **Can the Pickles:** Pack hot pickles into clean, hot pint jars. Add a piece of cinnamon stick to each jar. Cover with boiling syrup, leaving ½ inch headspace. Remove air bubbles, wipe jar rims, and adjust two-piece metal canning lids.
6. **Process and Seal Jars:** Adhere to altitude-specific processing times, then cool for 12–24 hours and verify seals.

WATER BATH CANNING ALTITUDE ADJUSTMENT CHART AND PROCESS TIME				
Style of Pack	Jar Size	0-1000 Ft	1001-6000 Ft	Above 6,000 Ft
Hot	Pints	10 min	15	20

32. PEAR PICKLES

INGREDIENTS:

» 4 lb Bartlett pears or another pickling pear (Bosc and Anjou varieties work well too)
» 1 cup water
» 4 cups sugar

» 2 cups apple cider vinegar (5%)
» 1 tbsp whole cloves
» 1 tbsp whole allspice berries
» 4 cinnamon sticks

Yield: About 3–4 pint

INSTRUCTIONS:

1. Boil a mix of sugar, vinegar, water, and cinnamon sticks in a pot. Add the cloves and allspice wrapped in a thin cloth and boil for 25 minutes.
2. Clean the pears, peel them, and remove the blossom ends. You can leave the stems on if you like. Cut large pears into halves or quarters. To keep the peeled pears from turning brown, place them in a cold solution made with ½ tsp ascorbic acid per 2 quarts of water. Drain them just before you're ready to use them.
3. Add the drained pears to the hot syrup, bring to a boil, then lower the heat and simmer for an additional 20 minutes.
4. Place the hot pears in the hot pint jars with a piece of cinnamon stick each. Cover with the hot syrup, leaving a space of about ½-inch space at the top of the jar.
5. Remove air bubbles, adjust headspace, clean the jar rims, and seal with lids. Process jars using boiling water canning guidelines.

This recipe is great for preserving pears in a sweet, spiced syrup, perfect for enjoying the fruit's flavor year-round.

WATER BATH CANNING ALTITUDE ADJUSTMENT CHART AND PROCESS TIME					
Style of Pack	Jar Size	0-1000 Ft	1001-3000 Ft	3,001-6,000Ft	Above 6,000 Ft
Hot	Pints	20 min	25	30	35

33. SWEET AND TANGY WATERMELON RIND PICKLES

INGREDIENTS:

- » 3 lb watermelon rind
- » 6 tbsp pickling salt
- » 6 cups water, plus additional for boiling
- » 3 cups granulated sugar
- » 1 ½ cups white vinegar (5%)

- » 1 ½ tbsp cinnamon sticks, broken up
- » 2 tsp whole cloves
- » 3/4 lemon, thinly sliced
- » 7–8 maraschino cherries, halved (optional)
- » 1 tbsp coriander seeds

Yield: About 2–3 pints

INSTRUCTIONS:

1. Remove the dark green and pink parts from the watermelon rind and discard them.
2. Cube the remaining rind into 1-inch pieces to make about 21 cups.
3. Soak the rind in a large container with the pickling salt and 6 cups of water. Add more water to cover the rind fully. Let it sit overnight.
4. Drain and thoroughly rinse the rind.
5. Simmer the rinsed rind in fresh cold water in a large saucepan until tender, about 10 minutes.
6. In a large pot, combine the sugar, vinegar, cinnamon sticks, cloves, and the remaining 3 cups of water. Let this syrup simmer for 10 minutes.
7. Add the watermelon rind, lemon slices, and optional maraschino cherries to the syrup. Simmer until the rind becomes translucent, about 30 minutes.
8. Pack the mixture into pint jars, leaving a 1/2-inch headspace. Seal the jars with lids.
9. Process the jars in a boiling water bath for 10 minutes, then remove them and let them cool on a rack.

WATER BATH CANNING ALTITUDE ADJUSTMENT CHART AND PROCESS TIME				
Style of Pack	Jar Size	0-1000 Ft	1001-6000 Ft	Above 6,000 Ft
Hot	Pints	10 min	15	20

34. PICKLED CANTALOUPE WITH A SWEET AND TANGY FLAVOR

INGREDIENTS:

» 9 lb (3 large or 4–5 medium ripe but firm) melons (like cantaloupe, canary or honeydew)
» 1 ½ cups water
» 1 ¼ cups white wine vinegar
» 3 cups sugar
» ½ cup chopped fresh mint
» 1 ½ tsp crushed red chili pepper
» 1 ½ tsp fine sea salt

Yield: About 4–5 pints jars

INSTRUCTIONS:

1. With a melon baller scoop out 9 cups of melon balls. Place them in a bowl and set aside any extra melon for other uses.
2. In a nonreactive saucepan, combine sugar, water, vinegar, and mint. Boil over medium-high heat, stirring until sugar dissolves. Remove from heat, cover, and let it steep for 1 hour. Then, strain the liquid and return it to the saucepan.
3. Add salt and crushed red pepper to the liquid and bring it to a boil again.
4. Tightly pack the melon balls into the jars. Pour the hot brine over them, leaving a 1/2-inch headspace. Ensure the melon balls are fully submerged. Gently jiggle the jars to settle the melon balls.
5. Secure the lids and process the jars in a boiling-water canner, see guidelines. Store the sealed jars in a cool, dark place for at least 1 week before serving. The pickled melon will keep for up to 6 months but may lose crispness over time. Refrigerate any jars that don't seal properly and use those first.

This recipe offers a delightful combination of sweet, tangy, and spicy flavors, perfect for enhancing fruit salads or as a unique addition to antipasto platters.

WATER BATH CANNING ALTITUDE ADJUSTMENT CHART AND PROCESS TIME				
Style of Pack	Jar Size	0-1000 Ft	1001-6000 Ft	Above 6,000 Ft
Hot	Pints	25 min	30	35

35. HONEY-SPICED ORANGES

INGREDIENTS:

- » 5 lb oranges
- » 6 tbsp lemon juice
- » 2 ½ cups granulated sugar
- » 6 cinnamon sticks
- » 3 tsp whole cloves
- » 3 tsp whole allspice
- » 2 ½ cups liquid honey
- » Water

Yield: About 3–4 pints

INSTRUCTIONS:

1. Make a spice bag with cinnamon stick pieces, cloves, and allspice in cheesecloth and set it aside.
2. Slice oranges into halves and thin slices, discarding ends and seeds. Place them in a large stainless-steel saucepan, cover with water, and boil. Then simmer until the peel is tender, about 15 minutes. Drain and keep aside.
3. In a separate saucepan, heat sugar, honey, and lemon juice until boiling, stirring to dissolve the sugar. Add the spice bag and orange slices. Boil again, then simmer until the oranges are glazed, about 40 minutes. Remove and discard the spice bag.
4. Get the boiling water canner, warm the jars in water that's just simmering (avoid boiling), and wash the lids in soapy water. Set the bands aside for later use.
5. Use a slotted spoon to fill jars with hot oranges, leaving 1/2-inch headspace. Ladle hot syrup over oranges, maintaining the same headspace. Tap jars to release air bubbles. Wipe jar rims, place lids, and tighten bands to fingertip tight.
6. Process jars in the boiling water canner for 10 minutes, adjusting for altitude. Turn off the heat, let jars sit for a few minutes in the canner, then cool jars for 12–22 hours. Finally, check the lids for seal; they shouldn't flex when pressed in the middle.

WATER BATH CANNING ALTITUDE ADJUSTMENT CHART AND PROCESS TIME				
Style of Pack	Jar Size	0-1000 Ft	1001-6000 Ft	Above 6,000 Ft
Hot	Pints	10 min	15	20

36. TANGY PEACH PICKLES

INGREDIENTS:

- » 4 lb small to medium-sized peaches (peeled)
- » 2 cups vinegar (5%)
- » 6 cups sugar
- » 2 sticks cinnamon
- » ½ tbsp ground ginger or (grated fresh ginger)
- » 1 tbsp crushed whole cloves

Yield: About 3 pints

INSTRUCTIONS:

1. Start by cleaning and peeling your peaches.
2. Place your spices into a small bag made of cheesecloth.
3. In a sizable pot, combine vinegar and sugar with your spice-filled cheesecloth bag. Heat this mixture until it reaches a boil, then continue boiling for five minutes.
4. Carefully boil the peaches in this syrup until they are tender enough to be pierced with a fork, but not too soft.
5. After boiling, remove from heat and let the peaches rest in the pickling liquid overnight in the fridge to become plump.
6. The next day, bring the peach and liquid mixture to a boil again. Then, remove the bag with spices.
7. Place the hot peaches into sterilized jars, and pour the hot liquid over them, ensuring to leave a ¼-inch space at the top.
8. Release any trapped air bubbles. Secure the jars with their lids.
9. Process the jars in a boiling water canner for 20 minutes, regardless of whether you're using pint or quart jars, according to the guidelines in the table's guidelines.
10. Once done, turn off the heat of the canner, remove its lid, and wait for 5 minutes before taking out the jars.

WATER BATH CANNING ALTITUDE ADJUSTMENT CHART AND PROCESS TIME					
Style of Pack	Jar Size	0-1000 Ft	1001-3000 Ft	3,001-6,000Ft	Above 6,000 Ft
Hot	Pints	20 min	25	30	35

37. PICKLED PLUMS WITH RED ONIONS

INGREDIENTS:

» 5 lb medium-sized red, purple, and/or green plums (around 21 plums)
» 3 medium red onions
» 3 cups red wine vinegar
» 3 cups water
» 1 tsp salt

» 3 cinnamon sticks
» 3 ½ cups sugar
» 6 whole cloves
» 3–4-star anise pods
» 12 whole allspices berries
» 2 bay leaves

Yield: About 7–8 pints

INSTRUCTIONS:

1. Rinse the plums, cut them in half, and remove the pits. Trim the ends from the onions and slice them into 1/2-inch-thick rings. Pack the plum halves and onion slices into hot, sterilized pint canning jars.
2. In a large stainless-steel saucepan, bring the water and red wine vinegar to a boil. Add sugar, cinnamon sticks, salt, allspice, star anise, and cloves. Stir until the sugar is fully dissolved, then remove from heat.
3. Carefully pour the hot vinegar mixture over the plums and onions in the jars, ensuring a ¼-inch headspace. Wipe the jar rims clean and place the lids on the jars.
4. Process the jars in a boiling-water canner for 20 minutes (start timing after the water returns to a boil). Remove the jars and let them cool on wire racks.
5. Refrigerate any jars that do not properly seal. Store the sealed jars in a cool, dark place for up to 6 months.

WATER BATH CANNING ALTITUDE ADJUSTMENT CHART AND PROCESS TIME				
Style of Pack	Jar Size	0-1000 Ft	1001-6000 Ft	Above 6,000 Ft
Raw	Pints	20 min	25	30

This recipe for pickled plums with red onions is deliciously sweet sour and spicy, ideal for enriching a variety of dishes.

38. BITTERSWEET SPICED PLUM PICKLES

INGREDIENTS:

» 3 lb firm-but-ripe plums
» 1 ½ cups distilled white vinegar
» 3 cups unseasoned rice vinegar
» ¾ cup pickling salt
» 3 cups dark brown sugar

» 2 cinnamon sticks, broken into 6 pieces (each pint jar)
» 6-star anise pods
» 1 ½ tsp fennel seeds
» 3 tsp pink peppercorns
» 12 cloves

Yield: About 6 pints

INSTRUCTIONS:

1. Wash the plums well by pitting them and cutting them into eight wedges each
2. In a saucepan, combine both vinegars with the brown sugar and salt, and bring the mixture to a boil to dissolve the sugar and salt. Using the sterilized tongs, remove the already sterilized jars from the hot water and transfer them to a rimmed baking sheet.
3. Pack the plums, cloves, star anise, broken cinnamon 4 pieces, peppercorns, and fennel seeds into the jars, leaving ½ inch of space at the top. Pour the hot brine over the plums, stopping ½ inch from the top. Screw the lids and rings on the jars securely but not too tightly.
4. Process the filled jars in a boiling-water canner for 20 minutes (start timing once the water returns to a boil).
5. Afterward, remove the jars from the canner and allow them to cool on wire racks.
6. Refrigerate any jars that do not seal. Store the sealed jars in a cool, dark place for up to 6 months.

WATER BATH CANNING ALTITUDE ADJUSTMENT CHART AND PROCESS TIME				
Style of Pack	Jar Size	0-1000 Ft	1001-6000 Ft	Above 6,000 Ft
Raw	Pints	20 min	25	30

This recipe has a unique touch by pickling fresh plums in a tasty and spicy brine that balances sweet and salty notes. A creative tip is to use these pickled plums to prepare a delicious soda. Simply blend the plums with their spicy pickling juice and a splash of sparkling water for a refreshing drink, topped with a sprig of basil for an aromatic touch.

39. PICKLED GINGER, JAPANESE STYLE

INGREDIENTS:

- » 2 lb young ginger rhizomes
- » 3 cups rice vinegar (or apple cider vinegar)
- » 2 cups granulated or cane sugar
- » 9 cups water
- » 2 tsp pickling salt

Yield: About 1–2 pints

INSTRUCTIONS:

1. Prepare ginger: Wash the ginger and trim any pink shoots, reserving them for later use. Cut the ginger into smaller pieces for easier handling. Peel it using a spoon and thinly slice it, either with a sharp knife or a mandolin.
2. Cook ginger: Boil a pot of water. Add the ginger slices and let them cook for about 3 minutes once the water returns to a boil. Then drain and set aside.
3. Make brine: In a steel pot, combine the rice vinegar, sugar, salt, and the pink shoots you set aside earlier. Heat the mixture over medium heat until the sugar and salt dissolve. Bring it to a boil; then, turn off the heat.
4. Dry ginger: After the ginger has cooled a bit, gently press it to remove excess water without squeezing too hard.
5. Jar and marinate: Place the ginger in sterilized jars. Pour the brine over the ginger, ensuring it is completely submerged. Let it cool, then refrigerate for at least 24 hours before using.
6. Storage: The pickled ginger can be stored in the refrigerator for up to 1 month.
7. Serving suggestions: This pickled ginger is perfect with sushi rice, cucumber sushi rolls, pickled radish, fried tofu pocket sushi, hand rolls, or other Japanese dishes. It's also great as a condiment for hot dogs or to add a zesty flavor to stir-fries, soups, and more.

Note: Young ginger, harvested in early summer, is ideal for this recipe. Look for ginger with pinkish tips for a natural color. You can usually find it in Asian grocery stores. This type of ginger is softer and has a milder flavor compared to the mature ginger typically used for cooking

40. CHERRIES PICKLED WITH SPICES

INGREDIENTS:

- » 2 lb fresh cherries, stemmed and pitted
- » 3 cups apple cider vinegar (5%)
- » 2 tsp pickling salt
- » 5–7 sprigs fresh thyme

- » 1 ½ cups brown sugar
- » 2 tsp fennel seeds
- » 2 bay leaves
- » 4 tsp whole black peppercorns
- » ½ tsp red pepper flakes (optional)

Yield: About 4 pints

INSTRUCTIONS:

1. Prepare jars and cherries: Distribute cherries evenly into 4 pint-sized glass jars (or 2 quart-sized jars) sterilized and interspersed with sprigs of thyme. Leave them to the side.
2. Create brine: In a medium-high heat saucepan, mix ¾ cup of water, vinegar, sugar, salt, peppercorns, fennel seeds, red pepper flakes, and a bay leaf. Heat the mixture until it boils, ensuring the sugar dissolves completely. Then, lower the heat and let it simmer for around 5–7 minutes.
3. Add brine to cherries: Once the brine is ready, pour it over the cherries in the jars, leaving about 1 inch of space at the top. You can strain the brine through a fine mesh sieve before pouring it if you prefer a less intense flavor.
4. Remove air bubbles and clean: After filling the jars, remove air bubbles by gently pressing the cherries against the side of the jar. Clean the jar edges with a damp cloth for a good seal.
5. Cool and store: Seal the jars and allow them to cool to room temperature. Once cooled, store them in the refrigerator.

Notes: The pickled cherries are best enjoyed after at least 24 hours of pickling.

Store the pickled cherries in the refrigerator, covered, for up to 3 weeks.

41. BERRY PICKLE WITH A SWEET AND SOUR TASTE

INGREDIENTS:

- » 3 cups assorted berries, such as (strawberries, blueberries, cherries, or raspberries)
- » 1 ½ cups apple cider vinegar (5%)
- » 3–6 tbsp sugar (adjust to taste)

- » 1 ½ tsp kosher salt
- » ½ cinnamon stick
- » 1–2-star anise pod
- » 1 spring thyme or several mint leaves
- » 2 cloves

Yield: About 1–2 pints

INSTRUCTIONS:

1. Prepare the Berries: Distribute the berries into two heat-proof jars, like canning jars.
2. Create the brine: In a medium-sized pot, bring the apple cider vinegar, sugar, salt, and 1 cup of water to a boil over high heat. Stir for 1–2 minutes until the sugar and salt dissolve.
3. Infuse flavor: Lower the heat to medium-low, add your choice of pickle seasonings, and let it simmer for another 1–2 minutes.
4. Combine and cool: Take the pot off the heat and let it cool a bit. Using tongs, transfer the seasonings into the jars with the berries. Then, pour the hot brine over the berries. Let the jars cool to room temperature.
5. Chill and serve: Cover the jars and refrigerate for at least 2 hours before serving. The pickled berries can be stored in a sealed container in the fridge for up to a week.

Notes: Savor the sweet-savory mix of this pickled berries recipe, great with any berries like blueberries, strawberries, raspberries, or cherries. While softer berries might turn into a spreadable form, adding a tangy touch to sandwiches, these pickled berries also excel as a condiment for roasted meats, cheese boards, or as a creative addition to cocktails.

42. STRAWBERRY JAM WITH LAVENDER AND HONEY

INGREDIENTS:

» 2 ¼ lb fresh strawberries
» 1 1/3 cups or (1 lb) honey

» 2 tbsp balsamic vinegar
» 2 tbsp dried lavender
» 1 lemon, juiced

Yield: About 2–3 pints

INSTRUCTIONS:

1. Berry preparation: Thoroughly rinse strawberries, trim off stems, and slice them into smaller pieces (halves or quarters).
2. Jar sterilization: Use a canning pot to sterilize the jar.
3. Jam thickness Test Setup: Put a small plate in your freezer for later testing the jam's thickness.
4. Jam making: Combine the strawberries and honey in a large, heavy-bottomed pot. Heat until it boils, then continue boiling for about 20–25 minutes until it thickens and the berries soften. Optionally, add herbs and balsamic vinegar and boil for an extra 8–10 minutes.
5. Consistency check: To test if the jam is ready, put a small spoonful on the chilled plate and swipe through it with your finger. If the jam stays separated, it's done. If not, continue boiling and retest in 8–10 minutes. Remove herb stems and turn off the heat.
6. Filling and sealing the jars: Carefully fill the sterilized jar with the hot jam. Place the lid on and twist the ring until snug but not overly tight. Process the jar in a hot water bath for 15 minutes.
7. Cooling and storing: Let the jar cool for 24 hours. The lid should seal itself (indicated by a depression in the middle). Store the sealed jar outside the fridge for up to a year. Refrigerate after opening.

Enjoy the delightful combination of lavender, balsamic vinegar, and honey in this strawberry preserve.

43. RHUBARB PICKLES

INGREDIENTS:

» 1 cup rhubarb, sliced diagonally into ¼-inch-thick pieces
» ½ cup apple cider vinegar
» ½ cup water
» ¼ cup to ½ cup sugar (adjusted to your preference)

» 2 ½ tsp Kosher salt
» 1 bay leaf
» 1 whole garlic clove
» 1 tsp fennel seeds
» 4 black peppercorns

Yield: About 1 pint

INSTRUCTIONS:

1. Start by preparing a brine with vinegar, water, sugar, salt, fennel seeds, bay leaf, garlic clove, and peppercorns. Bring the mixture to a boil until the sugar and salt dissolve. Once done, remove it from the heat and allow it to cool slightly.
2. Meanwhile, take the sliced rhubarb place it in a sterilized jar, and carefully pour in the lukewarm brine, filling the jar to the brim.
3. Seal the jar with a lid and let it sit at room temperature for 24 hours to cure.
4. Store the pickles in the refrigerator, where they can be kept for a few weeks.

44. QUICK GRAPES PICKLES

INGREDIENTS:

- » 2-pound grapes red or green
- » 2 cups red wine vinegar
- » 2 cups apple cider vinegar
- » 4 cups water
- » 4-inches ginger root

- » 1 cup brown sugar
- » 2 tbsp pickling salt
- » 4 tbsp mustard seeds
- » 4 whole cinnamon sticks
- » 2 bay leafs
- » 2 tsp whole black peppercorn

Yield: About 2 pints

INSTRUCTIONS:

1. Prepare the grapes: Wash and remove the grapes from the stems. You can choose to pickle them whole or halve them for a more intense flavor infusion from the pickling brine.
2. Get the pickling jar ready: Place the grapes, ginger, cinnamon sticks, and mustard seeds into a sterilized large jar.
3. Create and add the brine: In a saucepan, heat the water, red wine vinegar, apple cider vinegar, salt, and sugar until it reaches a boil. Then, pour this boiling mixture over the grapes in the jar, ensuring they are fully covered by the liquid, leaving a ½–1-inch space under the lid. Fasten the lid of the jar tightly.
4. Pickling process: Allow the jar to cool on the kitchen counter until it reaches room temperature. Once cooled, transfer the jar to the refrigerator and let the grapes pickle for a minimum of 2 hours before serving.
5. For optimal flavor, it's recommended to wait at least 24 hours before serving. These pickled grapes can be enjoyed for up to a month when stored in the refrigerator.

Pickled grapes present a treat adored by all. Infuse your toasts and salads with their delicious flavor. Enjoy these pickled grapes as a complement to salads, on toast, or as a delicious addition to a cheese plate!

45. AVOCADO PICKLES

INGREDIENTS:

- » 2 firm, slightly yielding fresh avocados
- » 1 1/3 cups water
- » 1 cup white balsamic vinegar
- » 2 tbsp honey
- » 1 tbsp pickling salt

- » 2 tsp dried red pepper
- » 6 garlic cloves, peeled and thinly sliced
- » 3 tsp peppercorns
- » 2 very thin lemon slices
- » 2 sprigs rosemary

Yield: About 1–2 pints

INSTRUCTIONS:

1. Prepare brine: In a medium saucepan, mix the vinegar, water, salt, and honey. Bring the mixture to a boil, stirring until the salt dissolves. Remove from heat and let it cool completely.
2. Jar preparation: Place the peppercorns, crushed red pepper, and garlic slices into a jar large enough to accommodate the increased quantity (likely a quart-sized jar).
3. Avocado preparation: Slice each avocado in half lengthwise, remove the seed, and peel while keeping the halves intact. Slice them widthwise into ½-inch pieces. Place the avocado slices into the prepared jar.
4. Adding flavor: Pour the cooled brine over the avocado slices in the jar. Tuck the rosemary sprig and lemon slices into the jar.
5. Seal and refrigerate: Secure the jar lid tightly. Refrigerate the jar for at least 5–6 hours.
6. Serving: Once the avocado slices are removed from the brine, they are versatile for various dishes. Try them in sandwiches or tossed in salads for an added zing. Alternatively, enjoy them solo for a quick snack. They also go great with creamy dips like tzatziki or guacamole, served with crispy tortilla chips or crusty bread. For a different twist, pair them with grilled chicken or fish, adding a tangy flair to your meal.

CHAPTER 10
CHUTNEY—RELISH—SALSA RECIPES

Chutney

Chutney is a popular relish-style condiment that has gained popularity due to the fusion of global flavors in Western cuisine. It originates from traditional East Indian cuisine and can be made with various ingredients, including herbs, fruits, and vegetables.

Fruit-based chutneys are typically cooked and can be canned or refrigerated, while others, like cilantro, onion, and coconut chutneys, are often enjoyed fresh.

Common spices in fruit chutney include chili powder, red pepper flakes, ginger, garlic, turmeric, and curry powder.

Chutney can be used in various ways, such as accompanying East Indian dishes, as a side, sandwich spread, dip, or flavor enhancer for everyday meals.

A balanced sweet and spicy chutney could go well with cheese, roasted meat, grilled chicken, or sandwiches. Since tastes vary, offering different chutney options might help everyone find their favorite. Keep in mind that chutney is not as common as in other culinary cultures.

Crafting chutney is a simple endeavor, but occasional blunders can crop up. Beyond the risk of scorching, challenges might emerge in storage practices.

Two primary concerns warrant attention:

1. **Prioritizing ingredient freshness** is pivotal. Just as with any recipe, opting for the freshest ingredients ensures impeccable flavor. Choose unblemished fruits, and always discard deceptive pieces.
2. **Careful cooking** is essential. Chutney, a delicate blend of fruits and vegetables, can occasionally scorch. Vigilant monitoring during medium-low heat cooking, with occasional stirring, prevents unwanted burn.

Moreover, **utilize non-reactive cookware**. Chutney's acidic components can react with certain metals, imparting an undesirable metallic taste. By using appropriate utensils, this issue can be avoided.

When these steps are well-executed, the likelihood of setbacks diminishes. However, if missteps occur, they often revolve around two key aspects:

Jar contraction: If store-bought chutney shrinks slightly after breaking the airtight seal, your homemade counterpart should exhibit similar behavior upon opening. If contraction persists with a sealed lid, troubleshooting is essential. Always verify a secure seal within 24 hours of processing.

Excess liquid: Should liquid pool atop the chutney after cooking, it indicates incomplete cooking. However, this can be rectified. If excess liquid is observed, return the chutney to the pot, cook until the surplus evaporates, then proceed to re-jar and seal.

Following these recommendations and tackling possible challenges, you can craft a delightful and flawless chutney. Moreover, it's recommended to allow the chutney to mature for a couple of months before consuming. During this period, the vinegar's acids work to soften the ingredients, and the fruit flavors blend and develop a heightened complexity.

Chutney and relish share many similarities. Both are crafted from fruits or vegetables, incorporating vinegar, sugar, and spices. However, their divergence lies primarily in texture. Relish retains its crunch and texture as the ingredients are cooked within the spiced vinegar. In contrast, chutney is typically slow-cooked until its components soften and meld together. This extended cooking process lends chutney a denser consistency compared to the looser texture of relish.

46. APPLE TOMATO CHUTNEY

INGREDIENTS:

- » 3 lb chopped tomatoes, peeled and chopped
- » 2 ½ lb apples, peeled, cored, and chopped, ideal (Granny Smith, Honeycrisp, or Pink Lady)
- » 1 cup chopped onion
- » 2 1/3 cups brown sugar
- » 1 cup seedless white raisins
- » ½ cup chopped green bell pepper
- » 2 cups cider vinegar (5%)
- » 2 tsp canning salt
- » ½ tsp ground ginger
- » 1 tsp mustard seeds
- » 2 tbsp whole mixed pickling spice

Yield: About 3–4-pint jars

Before commencing, please ensure to consult the guidelines on Using Boiling Water Canners, especially if you are new to canning. It is advisable to also read the Principles of Home Canning for foundational knowledge.

INSTRUCTIONS:

1. Initiate the process by thoroughly washing the tomatoes. Carefully peel and then chop them. Similarly, clean, peel, and chop the apples, ensuring to remove seeds and cores.
2. In a large mixing vessel, amalgamate all the ingredients, barring the whole spices. Encapsulate these spices in a clean, white cloth, securing it with a string, and then immerse it in the tomato and apple mixture. Proceed to heat the mixture until it reaches a vigorous boil. Maintain a gentle boil, stirring with regularity, until the mixture notably thickens and its volume reduces by approximately half, which should take around one hour. Following this, remove and discard the spice bag.
3. Carefully transfer the hot chutney into prepared pint jars, ensuring to leave ½ inch of space at the top. Eliminate any air bubbles and adjust the headspace as necessary. Clean the rims of the jars with a moistened, clean paper towel. Securely fasten the two-piece metal canning lids. The final step involves processing the jars in a Boiling Water Canner as per the canning guidelines.

WATER BATH CANNING ALTITUDE ADJUSTMENT CHART AND PROCESS TIME				
Style of Pack	Jar Size	0-1000 Ft	1001-6000 Ft	Above 6,000 Ft
Hot	Pints	10 min	15	20

47. CRANBERRY ORANGE CHUTNEY WITH A TANG

INGREDIENTS:

» 1 ½ cups fresh whole cranberries about (12 ounces)
» 1 cup golden raisins
» 1 cup cider vinegar (5%)
» ½ cup orange juice
» 1 tsp orange zest

» 1 ½ cups brown sugar
» 1 cup chopped white onion
» 2 tsp peeled, grated fresh ginger
» 1 stick cinnamon
» 1 tsp whole cloves
» 2-star anise

Yield: Approximately 4 half-pint jars.

INSTRUCTIONS:

1. Clean the cranberries meticulously. In a large saucepan or Dutch oven, mix all the ingredients. Heat the mixture until it boils, then lower the heat and let it simmer for 15 minutes or until the cranberries become soft. Constant stirring is essential to avoid burning. Afterward, remove and dispose of the cinnamon sticks and star anise.
2. Before using, ensure that the pint canning jars are thoroughly washed, rinsed, and kept heated. Lids should be prepared following the manufacturer's instructions.
3. Ladle the hot chutney into the prepared, warm pint jars, leaving a ½-inch space at the top. Release any trapped air bubbles and readjust the headspace as necessary. Clean the jar rims with a moistened, clean paper towel, then securely place the two-piece metal canning lids.
4. Process the jars in a boiling water canner, adhering to the time and method specified in the table's guidelines. After processing, allow the jars to cool undisturbed for 12–24 hours, and then check the seals for tightness.

WATER BATH CANNING ALTITUDE ADJUSTMENT CHART AND PROCESS TIME				
Style of Pack	Jar Size	0-1000 Ft	1001-6000 Ft	Above 6,000 Ft
Hot	Half-Pints	10 min	15	20

48. APPLE CHUTNEY WITH SWEET AND SPICY FLAVORS

INGREDIENTS:

» 8 cups apples (about 5 medium) such as Granny Smith, Honeycrisp, or Pink Lady apple
» ½ cup chopped sweet red bell peppers (about ½ medium)
» 1 cup golden raisins
» 1 tsp seeded and finely chopped red Serrano pepper
» ½ cup chopped onions
» 2 cups cane sugar
» 2 cups apple cider vinegar (5%)
» ½ garlic clove, crushed
» 1 tbsp ground ginger
» 1 tsp pickling salt
» 1 ½ tbsp mustard seed
» 1 tsp ground allspice
» ½ tsp coriander

Yield: About 3 pints

Safety Note: While handling hot peppers, wear plastic or rubber gloves and avoid touching your face. If gloves are not worn, wash your hands thoroughly with soap and water before touching your face or eyes.

INSTRUCTIONS:

1. Begin by washing, selecting, and chopping the apples, ensuring that seeds and cores are removed. After washing half a sweet bell pepper, carefully remove the seeds and inner white membranes, and chop them.
2. Before use, ensure that the pint canning jars are thoroughly washed, rinsed, and kept heated. Lids should be prepared following the manufacturer's instructions.
3. In a large pot, mix all the prepared ingredients. Heat the mixture until it boils, then reduce the heat and let it simmer until it becomes thick, which should take about 45 minutes. Stir often to prevent the mixture from sticking.
4. Carefully ladle the hot chutney into the jars, maintaining a ½-inch headspace. Expel any air bubbles and adjust the headspace as required. Clean the jar rims with a dampened, clean paper towel, then place and adjust the canning lids.
5. Process the jars in a boiling water canner, following the guidelines in the table's guidelines.
6. Allow the jars to cool undisturbed for 12 to 24 hours and then check the seals for tightness.

WATER BATH CANNING ALTITUDE ADJUSTMENT CHART AND PROCESS TIME				
Style of Pack	Jar Size	0-1000 Ft	1001-6000 Ft	Above 6,000 Ft
Hot	Pints	10 min	15	20

49. PEAR CHUTNEY

INGREDIENTS:

- » 8 cups pears (Bartlett or Bosc)
- » 1 to 1 ½ cups brown sugar
- » ½ cup chopped onions
- » 2 ½ cups apple vinegar (5%)
- » ½ cup raisins

- » 1 tbsp chopped fresh ginger
- » ½ garlic clove, minced
- » ½ hot red pepper
- » 1 tsp Kosher salt
- » 2 tbsp mustard seed
- » ½ tsp ground coriander

Yield: About 3–4 pints

INSTRUCTIONS:

1. Begin by thoroughly washing the pears peel them and chop them finely.
2. Before using, ensure that the canning jars are thoroughly cleaned and rinsed, then keep them warm. Prepare the lids as per the manufacturer's instructions.
3. In a large sauce pot, combine all the ingredients.
4. Simmer the mixture gently until it achieves a thick consistency, a process that typically requires around 35–40 minutes. It's important to stir the mixture regularly to ensure that the chutney does not adhere to the bottom of the pot.
5. Carefully pour the hot chutney into hot jars, leaving a 1/2-inch headspace. Firmly adjust the caps.
6. Process the jars in a boiling water bath for 10 minutes, following the guidelines in the table's guidelines.
7. Once the processing is done, remove the canner from heat, take off the lid, and wait for 5 minutes before removing the jars.

Storage Note: If you plan to use the chutney right away, it is advisable to wait for 24 hours. It can be stored in the refrigerator for 4–6 weeks; once opened, it should be consumed within a month. After completing the water bath canning process, the chutney can be stored on a shelf for up to a year.

Note: If you prefer a milder chutney, you can remove the seeds from the hot pepper. It's advisable to use rubber gloves to prevent your hands from getting burned while handling the pepper.

WATER BATH CANNING ALTITUDE ADJUSTMENT CHART AND PROCESS TIME				
Style of Pack	Jar Size	0-1000 Ft	1001-6000 Ft	Above 6,000 Ft
Hot	Pints	10 min	15	20

50. KIWI AND PEACH CHUTNEY WITH SPICES

INGREDIENTS:

»   2 cups firm-ripe kiwi, peeled and sliced thickly
»   3 cups sliced firm-ripe peaches or nectarines
»   ¼ cup fresh ginger root
»   1 ½ cups sugar
»   1 ½ cups cider vinegar (5%)
»   1 cup water

»   1 cup raisins
»   6 tbsp Worcestershire sauce
»   ½ cup finely chopped onion
»   ¾ cup lemon juice
»   ½ tsp pickling salt
»   ½ tsp ground cinnamon, ground allspice
»   ¼ tsp ground ginger, tsp cayenne pepper

Yield: About 3 pints

INSTRUCTIONS:

1. Start by covering the kiwi and peaches or nectarines with a saltwater solution (using 1 tbsp of salt per quart of water). Allow the fruits to sit in this solution overnight.
2. Chop the ginger and cook it until it becomes tender in 1 cup of water. Keep the cooking water aside.
3. In a pot, combine the sugar, vinegar, minced garlic, Worcestershire sauce, and the water used to cook the ginger. Cook this mixture until the sugar dissolves.
4. Drain the soaked fruits and add them to the sugar mixture. Cook until the nectarines become translucent, resembling the texture of preserves.
5. Separate the cooked fruit from the syrup and then add the remaining ingredients (onion, ground ginger, raisin, cinnamon, allspice, cayenne pepper) to the syrup. Cook until the onions turn soft, and the mixture reaches your desired thickness.
6. Reintroduce the cooked fruit to the syrup and bring the mixture to a boil. Taste and adjust the seasoning as necessary.
7. Carefully pour the chutney into sterilized canning jars, ensuring a ½ inch of space at the top. Seal the jars with lids.
8. Process the sealed jars in a boiling water canner for 10 minutes. follow the table's guidelines.
9. Once the processing is done, remove the canner from heat, take off the lid, and allow it to stand for 5 minutes before removing the jars.

Caution: When working with large quantities of kiwi, wear rubber gloves to avoid irritation to the skin.

WATER BATH CANNING ALTITUDE ADJUSTMENT CHART AND PROCESS TIME				
Style of Pack	Jar Size	0-1000 Ft	1001-6000 Ft	Above 6,000 Ft
Hot	Pints	10 min	15	20

51. FIG AND APPLE BALSAMIC CHUTNEY

INGREDIENTS:

- » 2 ½ cups large figs, stems removed and cut into eighths (8–12 figs)
- » 2 cups red apples, cored and roughly chopped
- » 1 ½ cups red onions, chopped
- » 1 tbsp olive oil
- » ½ cup red wine vinegar (at least 5% acetic acid)

- » 1 cup balsamic vinegar (at least 5% acetic acid)
- » ½ tsp nutmeg
- » 1 ½ cups muscovado sugar
- » 1 tsp mustard seeds
- » ½ tsp chili pepper
- » 1 tsp coriander seeds
- » ½ tsp cinnamon

Yield: Approximately 1–2 pints

INSTRUCTIONS:

1. Start by warming up some oil in a big skillet. Toss in onions and let them sweat it out until they're soft and have a nice, golden hue
2. Next, throw in those chopped apples and figs. Give it a good sprinkle of sugar and stir it all up until the sugar has melted away. Now, for the flavor kick—mix in some spice, nutmeg, cinnamon, red wine vinegar, and balsamic vinegar. Make sure everything's mixed in nicely.
3. Now, crank up the heat until it's bubbling, then dial it back and let it simmer for a good 30–45 minutes. Keep an eye on it and stir it every now and then.
4. About 25 minutes in, grab a masher and gently break up the bigger chunks. Keep simmering until it thickens up to how you like it.

If you want to savor this chutney: simply transfer it to a bowl. You may want to let it cool a bit first and then it is ready to be stored in the refrigerator. It will keep fresh for about 4–6 weeks. Remember, however, that once opened, you must consume it within a month for maximum flavor and freshness.

If storing in jars: Sterilize your clean jars in a water bath canner for 10 minutes.

1. Transfer the chutney into your jars whilst it is still hot and screw on the lids tightly (use a jam funnel for ease),
2. Carefully pour the chutney into sterilized canning jars, ensuring a ½ inch of space at the top. Seal the jars with lids.
3. Process the sealed jars in a boiling water canner for 10 minutes. follow the table's guidelines.
4. Once the processing is done, remove the canner from heat, take off the lid, and allow it to stand for 5 minutes before removing the jars. A vacuum seal will form as the chutney cools.

This red wine fig chutney is perfect with cheeses and red meats, such as game.

WATER BATH CANNING ALTITUDE ADJUSTMENT CHART AND PROCESS TIME				
Style of Pack	Jar Size	0-1000 Ft	1001-6000 Ft	Above 6,000 Ft
Hot	Pints	10 min	15	20

52. PUMPKIN AND CRANBERRY CHUTNEY WITH SPICES

INGREDIENTS:

- » 1-pound fresh cranberries
- » ½ lb Bramley apple, (2 medium) peeled, cored, and diced
- » 1 ½ lb diced lightly roasted pumpkin
- » 1 ¼ cups light brown sugar
- » 3 tsp sea salt
- » 2 ¼ cups apple cider vinegar
- » ½ cup fresh ginger, grated
- » 1 ½ tsp turmeric
- » 1 ½ tsp toasted cumin seeds (toasted in a dry pan)
- » 1 ½ tsp ground coriander
- » 1 red chili (optional)
- » ½ tsp dried chili flakes (optional)

INSTRUCTIONS:

1. Place all ingredients in a pot and heat until the mixture reaches a boil. Then, reduce the heat and let the mixture simmer, stirring constantly. Continue simmering until the chutney thickens slightly and the pumpkin becomes tender, stirring occasionally, about 50 minutes, or until the chutney has thickened slightly and the fruit is soft.
2. Carefully ladle the hot chutney into five sterilized pint jars, leaving about ½-inch of headspace at the top. Gently tap the jars to remove any trapped air bubbles, and if necessary, adjust the headspace by adding more hot chutney. Clean the rims of the jars with a clean, damp cloth. Center the lids on the jars and screw on the bands until fingertip tight.
3. Place the jars in a canner filled with simmering water, ensuring the jars are completely submerged. Increase the heat to bring the water to a full rolling boil and process the jars for 10 minutes. After processing, turn off the heat, remove the canner lid, and wait 5 minutes before carefully removing the jars. Allow the jars to cool completely in a cool. The chutney will be kept in a cool, dark place for several months.

It is delicious, especially with turkey, chicken, ham or roast pork

53. RHUBARB AND ORANGE CHUTNEY WITH A TANG

INGREDIENTS:

- » 3 1/3 lb chopped fresh rhubarb
- » 3 chopped onions (medium)
- » 2–3 oranges freshly juiced and zested
- » 2 cups raisins
- » 4 ½ cups brown sugar

- » 4 cups cider vinegar (5%)
- » 1 ½ tbsp ginger root (chopped)
- » 1 ½ tbsp mustard seeds
- » 5 whole black peppercorns
- » 1 tsp coriander seed, red pepper flakes
- » 3 tsp curry powder

Yield: Approximately 4–5 pints

INSTRUCTIONS:

1. Prepare jars: Begin by sterilizing pint jars. Place the jars in boiling water and boil them for 10 minutes. After sterilizing, keep the jars warm until they are ready to be filled
2. Prepare spice bag: Enclose peppercorns, mustard seeds, coriander seeds, and red pepper flakes in a piece of gauze. Set aside.
3. Cook chutney: In a large stainless-steel saucepan, combine orange zest, orange juice, rhubarb, brown sugar, cider vinegar, onions, raisins, and ginger. Stir constantly and bring to a boil over medium-high heat. Reduce heat and gently simmer for 45–50 minutes while stirring occasionally.
4. Add spices: Incorporate curry powder and the spice bag. Simmer for another 30 minutes or until thick enough to mound up on a spoon.
5. Can chutney: Once ready gently pour the hot chutney into the preheated jars, leaving ½-inch headspace from the top. Remove air bubbles, wipe rims, and secure lids. Process in boiling water for 10 minutes. Adjust the time if you're at a different altitude. Cool jars for 5 minutes in the canner, then remove and let cool for 12–24 hours. Check seals.

Celebrate the fusion of rhubarb, raisins, and orange juice in this chutney, spiced with ginger, and curry. Perfect with curried veggies, papadum, or as a unique addition to your charcuterie board.

54. JALAPEÑO PINEAPPLE RELISH

INGREDIENTS:

» 4 cups diced pineapple, peeled (about 1 pineapple)
» 2–3 Jalapeño chopped and seeded
» ¾ cup red onion, finely chopped
» ¼ cups red pepper, finely chopped
» ½ cup fresh cilantro leaves only
» ½ cup apple cider vinegar
» ¼ cup brown sugar
» 1 tsp salt (or to taste)
» 1 lime juiced

Yield: About 2 pints

INSTRUCTIONS:

1. Prepare a pot for boiling water. Sterilize the jars in boiling water for 10 minutes, and leave them warm until ready to use. Wash the lids in warm soapy water and set them aside with the bands.
2. Finely chop the pineapple, red onion, and Jalapeño in a food processor. Aim for a chunky texture rather than a smooth puree, using just a few quick pulses.
3. Combine all other ingredients in a non-reactive saucepan on medium heat. Bring this mixture to a boil, then lower the heat for a 5-minute simmer. Next, stir in the pineapple mixture and simmer until the liquid is halved in volume, which should take about 20–25 minutes.
4. Transfer the hot relish into each jar, maintaining a ½-inch space from the top. After removing air bubbles and cleaning the rim of each jar, place the lid and gently screw on the band. Put each jar into the canner, repeating the process for all.
5. Allow the jars to process in the canner for 15 minutes, adjusting the timing based on altitude. Turn off the heat and remove the canner's lid, letting the jars rest for 5 minutes. Remove the jars and leave them to cool for 12–24 hours. Check that the lids have sealed correctly, ensuring they don't pop when pressed at the center.

Note: For safety, remember to wear gloves when handling hot peppers.

Perfectly complements Grilled Pork Chops, also amazing on burgers, hot dogs, chicken, or tacos.

WATER BATH CANNING ALTITUDE ADJUSTMENT CHART AND PROCESS TIME				
Style of Pack	Jar Size	0-1000 Ft	1001-6000 Ft	Above 6,000 Ft
Hot	Pints	15 min	20	25

55. MIXED PEPPERS RELISH

INGREDIENTS:

» 15 large bell peppers or 10 cups of ground (mix of red, yellow, and green) peppers
» 3 medium yellow onions or 1 ½ cups of ground onions
» 4 tsp pickling salt
» 2 ½ cups apple cider vinegar

» 2 cups granulated sugar
» 3 tsp yellow mustard seeds
» 2 tsp sweet Hungarian paprika
» 1 tsp garlic powder or fresh
» 1 tsp ground black pepper,

Yields: About 6-7 pint jars

INSTRUCTIONS:

1. Sterilize jars: Start by washing and rinsing pint canning jars, ensuring they remain hot until ready to be filled. Follow the manufacturer's instructions to prepare lids and ring bands.
2. Prepare the veggies: Clean and halve the bell peppers, removing seeds and ribs. Chop them into large pieces. Finely chop most of the peppers and coarsely chop half of the onions. Use a food processor for the rest.
3. Salt and ice treatment: Combining chopped peppers and onions with salt helps draw out moisture, enhancing the relish's texture. Cover with ice and refrigerate for 2–3 hours to crisp up the vegetables.
4. Cooking the relish: Drain and squeeze out moisture from the pepper-onion mix. In a pot, mix the vinegar, sugar, mustard seeds, paprika, and the added spices. Add the drained veggies and boil. Simmer for about 40–50 minutes until thickened.
5. Jar filling: Pour hot dressing into preheated jars leaving 1/2-inch space. Remove air bubbles, adjust headspace, and wipe edges to ensure a secure seal.
6. Canning process: Seal with the lids, then place in boiling water for 10 minutes. Adjust for altitude if necessary, following the recommendations provided in the table's guidelines. After processing, allow jars to cool undisturbed for 12–24 hours, then check for proper sealing.

WATER BATH CANNING ALTITUDE ADJUSTMENT CHART AND PROCESS TIME				
Style of Pack	Jar Size	0-1000 Ft	1001-6000 Ft	Above 6,000 Ft
Hot	Pints	10 min	15	20

Pickled Eggs

Safety First: Storing Pickled Eggs

Before diving into the process of pickling eggs, it's crucial to understand the importance of proper storage. Pickled eggs must be refrigerated and should not be left at room temperature, except during serving, which should not exceed two hours within a temperature range of 40°F to 140°F. This precaution is due to the risk of botulism from eggs stored at room temperature. For detailed safety guidelines, refer to the CDC's official website.

Pickling Process

Use peeled, hard-cooked eggs in a boiling mixture of vinegar, salt, spices, and other seasonings. Boil the solution, simmer for 5 minutes, then pour over the eggs. Boiling solutions yield tender Egg whites.

Selecting and Preparing Eggs

- Choose eggs with clean shells. Smaller or medium-sized eggs are preferable for thorough seasoning.
- Use fresh eggs for better quality. Eggs a few days old are easier to peel after boiling.
- For easy peeling, especially of fresh eggs, make a pinhole in the larger end, boil, then transfer between hot and ice water. Peel under cold water.

Choosing Containers

Use airtight containers, like glass canning jars. Ensure eggs are fully covered in the pickling solution. A quart-sized jar can hold about a dozen medium eggs.

Seasoning and Consumption

After preparation, allow time for eggs to absorb the flavors, keeping them refrigerated. Small eggs take 1–2 weeks, and larger eggs 2–4 weeks. Consume within 3–4 months for best quality.

This summary provides the essential steps and safety tips for making pickled eggs, emphasizing proper handling and storage for safety and quality.

56. EGGS PICKLED WITH DILL

INGREDIENTS:

- 12 fresh eggs
- 1 cup water
- 1 ½ cups white vinegar
- 3 tsp salt
- ¼ tsp white pepper
- ¼ tsp mustard seed
- ¾ tsp dill weed
- 1 peeled minced garlic
- ½ tsp minced onion

Yield: About 2–3 pints /1-quart jar

INSTRUCTIONS:

1. Begin by placing the fresh eggs in cold water and bringing it to a point just before boiling. Reduce the heat and let the eggs simmer for 15 minutes.
2. Immediately transfer the cooked eggs to cold water and remove their shells.
3. Take a quart jar and sterilize it by boiling it in water for 10 minutes.
4. Pack the peeled eggs into the sterilized jar.
5. In a pot, combine the white vinegar, water, sugar, dill weed, white pepper, salt, mustard seed, and either onion juice or minced onion, as well as minced garlic or a peeled garlic clove. Bring the mixture to a boil, then reduce the heat and let it simmer for 5 minutes.
6. Carefully pour the hot liquid over the hard-cooked eggs in the jar.
7. Close the jar with an airtight lid and place the eggs in the refrigerator to marinate for at least 3 days before consuming. The flavor of pickled eggs will strengthen with time; let the eggs absorb the flavors in the refrigerator. Small eggs need 1–2 weeks, while medium to large eggs need 2–4 weeks for seasoning.

The best quality is achieved by consuming the eggs within 3–4 months.

57. PINEAPPLE AND SPICY PICKLED EGGS

INGREDIENTS:

- » 12 fresh eggs
- » 1 ½ cups pineapple juice (sugar-free),
- » (If using sweetened juice, do not add extra sugar)
- » 1 ½ cups cider vinegar (5%)
- » ¼ cup sugar

- » 2 medium onions, peeled and sliced
- » 1 tsp salt
- » ½ tsp red pepper flakes
- » 1 tsp coriander
- » ½ tsp whole cloves

Yield: About 2–3 pints / 1-quart jar

INSTRUCTIONS:

1. Begin by placing the fresh eggs in cold water and bringing it to a point just before boiling. Reduce the heat and let the eggs simmer for 15 minutes.
2. Immediately transfer the cooked eggs to cold water and remove their shells.
3. Take a quart jar and sterilize it by boiling it in water for 10 minutes.
4. Pack the peeled eggs into the sterilized jar.
5. In a pot, combine the cider vinegar, sugar, pineapple juice, salt, pepper flakes, coriander, cloves, and sliced onion. Bring the mixture to a boil, then reduce the heat and let it simmer for five minutes.
6. Carefully pour the hot liquid over the hard-cooked eggs in the jar.
7. Close the jar with an airtight lid and place the eggs in the refrigerator to marinate for at least 3 days before consuming. The flavor of pickled eggs will strengthen with time; let the eggs absorb the flavors in the refrigerator. Small eggs need 1–2 weeks, while medium to large eggs need 2–4 weeks for seasoning.

The best quality is achieved by consuming the eggs within 3–4 months.

58. PICKLED EGGS WITH RED BEET

INGREDIENTS:

» 12 fresh eggs
» 1 cup red beet juice (from canned beets)
» or slices beets can be used
» 1 tsp brown sugar
» 1 ½ cups cider vinegar
» ½ tsp Kosher salt
» ½ tsp black pepper
» 2 bay leaves

Yield: About 2–3 pints/ 1-quart jar

INSTRUCTIONS:

1. Begin by placing the fresh eggs in cold water and bringing it to a point just before boiling. Reduce the heat and let the eggs simmer for 15 minutes.
2. Immediately transfer the cooked eggs to cold water and remove their shells.
3. Take a quart jar and sterilize it by boiling it in water for 10 minutes.
4. Pack the peeled eggs into the sterilized jar.
5. In a pot, combine the cider vinegar, sugar, red beet juice, salt, black pepper, and bay leaves. Bring the mixture to a boil, then reduce the heat and let it simmer for five minutes.
6. Carefully pour the hot liquid over the hard-cooked eggs in the jar.
7. Close the jar with an airtight lid and place the eggs in the refrigerator to marinate for at least 3 days before consuming. The flavor of pickled eggs will strengthen with time; let the eggs absorb the flavors in the refrigerator. Small eggs need 1–2 weeks, while medium to large eggs need 2–4 weeks for seasoning.

The best quality is achieved by consuming the eggs within 3–4 months.

Meat and Fish

Preserving Meat Safely

This chapter is aimed at those who appreciate the importance of having ready-made and easy-to-serve meals, especially on busy evenings when time and energy are limited. You will learn how to turn basic ingredients like chicken, beef, and other types of meat into convenient pre-packaged options, perfect for times when cooking from scratch is not possible. The goal is to provide knowledge on how to effectively preserve meat, ensuring that it maintains its organoleptic and nutritional qualities.

In this journey of culinary preservation, we will delve into the specifics of canning, particularly focusing on meat, poultry, and game. It's vital to understand the importance of using a pressure canner for these types of low-acid foods. This method is not just a choice but a necessity for safe consumption. Through this chapter, we'll explore the reasons behind this requirement and how to correctly use a pressure canner, ensuring that your preserved meats are not only delicious but also safe to eat.

Follow these guidelines for processing:

- Use an 11-pound pressure for a dial gauge pressure canner.
- Utilize a 15-pound pressure for a weighted gauge pressure canner and adhere to the specified processing times.
- Maintain a high standard of cleanliness and efficiency during the handling process.

Remember these essential tips when canning meats:

1. Begin with properly cleaned and chilled meat.
2. Can fresh meat and poultry within 48 hours or freeze it for later use.
3. Process fish promptly or freeze it until you're ready to can.
4. Thaw frozen products in the refrigerator until most ice crystals have melted before proceeding with the canning process.
5. Before canning, remove the gristle and excess fat from the meat to avoid potential sealing issues caused by melted fat during processing.
6. While salt is optional, you may choose to add it to the canned meat or poultry.
7. For larger game animals like deer, follow the processing times and methods for beef.
8. For smaller game animals and birds, adhere to the processing times and methods typically used for poultry.

Equipment Needed for Pickling Meat at Home

- Brining pot or container: Choose a size suitable for your meat.
- Pressure canners now have safety features for a more secure experience.
- Storage containers: Use glass, plastic, or stainless-steel containers with airtight lids.
- Preparation tools: A cutting board and sharp knife.
- Handling tools: Tongs or a slotted spoon for safe meat handling.

To qualify as a pressure canner for USDA canning procedures, the canner must meet the following criteria:

1. For safe processing in a pressure canner, you must have at least 2-quart jars or 4-pint jars in each batch. This ensures the pressure and temperature reach the necessary levels for safe canning.
2. It must include a vent for releasing air from inside the canner while it is pressurized.
3. It must be equipped with a mechanism, such as a gauge or weighted gauge, to indicate and maintain the desired pressure level within the canner throughout the entire processing duration.

Safety First

Before starting the pressure canning process, ensure the safety of your equipment and jars. Check for appropriate jar temperatures and proper lid placement. If any issues are noticed, it's okay to remove the jars from the process.

Always prioritize safety by verifying the condition and safety features of your pressure canner. Conduct a small test batch, like canning a jar of soup, to validate the equipment's functionality and gain peace of mind. Your safety should always be the top concern.

59. RECIPE FOR CANNING MEAT; BEEF, PORK, AND MORE

EQUIPMENT:

» Wide-mouth jars (quart-sized, or pint-sized if preferred)
» A pressure canner
» Lids with rings
» Canning funnel
» One or two clean rags

INGREDIENTS:

» Cubed raw red meat (such as lamb, beef, pork, veal, venison or other wild game)
» 1 tsp salt for each quart jar (optional, for taste)
» Boiling water

RAW-PACK METHOD:
INSTRUCTIONS:

1. Begin by boiling water in your pressure canner.
2. Neatly pack cubed meat into jars, filling up to an inch below the top. Ensure the meat isn't too tightly packed to allow circulation of liquid.
3. Optionally, add 1 tsp of salt per quart jar, and ½ tsp if using one-pint jars.
4. Add boiling water to each jar, leaving some space at the top. Wipe the jar rims with a wet cloth, then dry them.
5. Check the jar rims by running a finger around them to remove any salt or bubbles, which can hinder sealing.
6. Place lids and rings on the jars and set them in your pressure canner.
7. Arrange jars on the canner's rack to avoid movement and potential breakage.
8. Heat the canner to build up pressure, keeping the weight gauge off initially.
9. Let the steam vent for 10 minutes before placing the weight. Wait for the pressure to reach 10 lb (adjust for altitude check the guidelines table).
10. Maintain this pressure for 90 minutes.
11. After 90 minutes, let the pressure reduce naturally. Once normalized, remove the jars and let them cool for 16–24 hours. Remove rings and clean jars if needed.

Notes:

Preheat your canner while preparing jars for efficiency.
Salt is optional and mainly for flavor, not preservation.
The quantity of meat determines the number of jars you'll need.
Ensure safety by turning off the heat while loading jars and using a rack.
Simply open a jar to add this meat to a variety of dishes, such as soups, stews, or sauces. This recipe offers clear, concise instructions for the home canning of meat, ensuring effective and safe preservation.

60. CANNING RECIPE FOR POULTRY; CHICKEN, TURKEY, AND MORE

This recipe outlines two safe methods for canning chicken: raw pack and hot pack. The raw pack method involves placing raw chicken pieces directly into jars, adding water and spices, then processing. For the hot pack method, chicken is partially cooked before being jarred and processed. Both ensure the chicken is thoroughly cooked during pressure canning, eliminating the need for precooking.

INGREDIENTS:

»   9 chicken breasts, cubed (you can also use duck, goose, or turkey)

»   3 tsp salt (optional)
»   1 ½ cups nearly boiling water

Yield: About 6 pints

INSTRUCTIONS:

Preparation Steps:

1.   Warm your pressure canner with moderately hot water and place a rack inside to prevent jar breakage. Keep jars warm inside the canner.
2.   Cube the chicken breasts into 1-inch cubes.

Canning Process:

1.   Take the jars out of the canner, making sure they are dry.
2.   Fill each jar with 2 cups of cubed chicken, leaving roughly 1 ¼ inches of headspace.
3.   Use tongs or a bubble remover tool to lightly press down the chicken, maintaining the right headspace.
4.   Add about ½ inch of hot water to each jar.
5.   Optionally, add the salt per jar for flavor enhancement.
6.   Wipe jar rims with a clean cloth moistened with hot water or vinegar for a secure seal.
7.   Apply the lids and screw on the bands until just tight.

Pressure Canning:

1.   Use jar lifters to place jars in the canner.
2.   Seal the canner lid according to the manufacturer's guidelines and heat in a medium setting.
3.   Allow steam to vent for 10 minutes to purge the canner of air.
4.   Place the pressure weight on the vent; adjust the pressure based on your canner model and altitude as per the chart.
5.   Increase pressure gradually and stabilize before timing the canning process. Process pints for 75 minutes and quarts for 90 minutes, adjusting for your specific method.

Cooling and Sealing:

1.   After the allotted time, turn off the heat and let the canner depressurize naturally.
2.   Once depressurized, remove the weight and open the canner.
3.   Carefully remove jars and place them on a towel on a draft-free surface to cool for 12–16 hours.
4.   Check the seal on each jar to ensure it is tight. Unsealed jars should be refrigerated and used promptly.
5.   Label the jars with the contents and canning date for organization.

Notes:

This recipe works for various types of poultry, with or without bones and skin.

Adding water helps prevent the meat from drying, improving texture and appearance without affecting safety.

Salt, while not essential for preservation, adds flavor. Other dry seasonings can be used, avoiding thickeners not safe for canning.

Canned chicken lasts 2–8 years on the shelf but for best quality, consumed within a year.

61. CANNED MEATBALLS IN SALSA

INGREDIENTS:

» 5 lb ground meat
» 2 cups fine breadcrumbs
» 1 tbsp garlic powder

» 4–5 cups hot tomato sauce
» 2 tbsp salt
» 2 tbsp dried parsley flakes

Yield: About 5 pints

INSTRUCTIONS:

1. In a large bowl, thoroughly mix all the ingredients using your hands. Shape the mixture into firm meatballs, sized to fit in your palm.
2. Cook them until lightly browned.
3. Place 4–5 meatballs into each sterilized pint jar, ensuring not to overfill, leaving room for sauce. Cover the meatballs with hot tomato sauce.
4. Gently use a spatula to remove air pockets, allowing the sauce to fill the jar, leaving 1 inch of headspace at the top.
5. Process for 75 minutes (pints) or 90 minutes (quarts) in a pressure canner at 10 lb of pressure, adjusting for altitude see the Table.

62. CANNED CHILI CON CARNE

INGREDIENTS:

- » 2 cups dried red kidney beans or pinto beans
- » 4 cups water
- » 2 tsp salt divided
- » 2 ¼ lb ground beef
- » 1 cup finely chopped onion
- » ½ cup chopped peppers of your choice (optional)
- » 1 tsp black pepper
- » 2–4 tbsp chili powder, to taste
- » 5 cups tomatoes, crushed or whole

INSTRUCTIONS:

1. Prepare canning equipment: Heat 2–3 inches of water in your pressure canner until it simmers. Sterilize your jars, lids, and bands.
2. Soak the beans: Clean the beans and soak them in a 2-quart pot with cold water covering them by three inches, for 16–20 hours.
3. To cook the beans: Drain the soaked beans, then add them to the pot with 4 cups of fresh water and a tsp of salt. Bring to a boil, reduce to a simmer for 30 minutes, then drain.
4. Cooking the chili: In a skillet, brown the ground beef, then add the onions and optional peppers, draining any excess grease. Stir in the black pepper, the rest of the salt, the chili powder, tomatoes, and the pre-cooked beans. Allow it to simmer together for about 5 minutes.
5. Canning the chili: Spoon the hot chili into your sterilized jars, leaving one inch of space at the top. Clean the jar rims, place the lids on, and tighten the bands moderately.
6. Processing: Set the jars in the canner, secure the lid, and let the pressure build. Vent steam for 10 minutes before adding the pressure weight.
7. Processing times: Adjust the canner to 11 lb of pressure for a dial-gauge canner, or 10 lb for a weighted-gauge canner, and process for 75 minutes. Adjust for altitude as needed.
8. After processing: Allow the canner to depressurize on its own, then remove the jars to cool for 12–16 hours. Check that the seals are tight, remove the bands, clean the jars, and store them.

Notes:

This recipe offers flexibility in bean and meat choices, accommodating various dietary preferences and tastes. Whether you opt for kidney beans, pinto beans, or another variety, the process remains the same. Similarly, while ground beef is standard, feel free to experiment with venison, lamb, or pork. The inclusion of peppers is up to your taste preference, with a mix of Poblano and Jalapeño peppers recommended for a moderate but flavorful heat level.

The following is the recommended **process time for meat** (chunk or cubes), **meatballs, chili con carne, poultry, and rabbit** in a dial-gauge pressure canner.

Style of pack	Jar Size	Process Time min	CANNER PRESSURE (PSI) AT ALTITUDES OF			
			0– 2,000 ft.	2,001– 4,000 ft.	4,001– 6,000 ft.	6,001– 8,000 ft.
Hot and Raw	Pints	75	11 lb	12 lb	13 lb	14 lb
	Quarts	90	11	12	13	14

The following is the recommended **process time for meat** (chunks or cubes**), poultry, and rabbit** in a weighted—gauge pressure canner.

Style of Pack	Jar size	Time Min	CANNER PRESSURE (PSI) AT ALTITUDES OF	
			0–1,000 ft.	Above 1,000 ft.
Hot and Raw	Pints	75	10 lb	15 lb
	Quarts	90	10	15

Seafood

Preserving fish safely

- To preserve fish safely, it is important to clean them quickly and choose between canning or pickling methods.
- Fresh fish is essential for successful preservation, as fish are prone to decomposition, rancidity, and microbial spoilage.
- Proper handling and immediate cleaning of the fish help minimize the risk of foodborne illnesses and maintain the quality of the meal.
- Sustaining the vitality of freshly caught fish is crucial.
- Spoilage and slime-producing bacteria are naturally present on every fish and multiply rapidly in warm water, so prompt cleaning is crucial.
- Fish spoil quickly, especially in higher temperatures, but the spoilage process slows down as temperatures approach freezing.
- The proper use of ice is crucial for preserving the freshness of fish.
- Fish should be packed in a cooler with a ratio of one lb of crushed ice for every 2 lb of fish.
- Fish stored at temperatures of 40°F or lower can retain quality for up to three days, depending on the initial quality of the fish and the refrigerator temperature.

By following these steps, you can preserve fish safely while maintaining their freshness and quality.

Canning Fish Safely

Fish, a low-acid food, requires high-temperature processing in a pressure canner for safety. Processing at temperatures below 240°F may not eliminate heat-resistant Clostridium botulinum spores, posing a risk of botulism, a serious toxin-induced illness. Even with the addition of vinegar or when fish is canned in tomato-based products, using a pressure canner is critical. Always use standard, heat-tempered canning jars for this process.

63. CANNED FISH RECIPE: TROUT, SALMON, BLUEFISH

INGREDIENTS:

- » 6–8 lb fish (trout, swordfish, mackerel, kokanee, salmon, and other fatty fish
- » 1 tsp pickling salt per pint jar (optional)
- » 2 tsp white vinegar per pint jar

Yield: 7–8 pints

INSTRUCTIONS:

1. Preparation: Bleed and gut the trout immediately after catching (within 2 hours) and chill on ice. Alternatively, use pre-cleaned fish. If frozen, thaw completely in the fridge.
2. Jar preparation: Remove trout heads and tails, cutting them into jar-sized pieces. Leave 1 inch of headspace; for half-pint jars, cut into 1 ½ inch chunks. Add ½ tsp of pickling salt and 1 tsp of white vinegar to each jar.
3. Packing jars: Place fish chunks in jars, keeping bones and skin intact. Wipe jar rims clean.
4. Pressure cooking: In the cooker, add 4 inches of water. Stack jars with dividers if needed. Lock the lid, leaving the steam vent open.
5. Venting and processing: Heat until steaming, then vent steam for 10 minutes. Cover the vent, increase pressure to 10 lb (adjust for altitude), and maintain for 100 minutes.
6. Cooling: Turn off the heat and let the cooker depressurize naturally. Once at zero pressure, remove jars to a cooling rack for 8–12 hours.
7. Post-processing: Remove rings, check seals, wash jars, label with date and contents, and store in a cool, dry place.

Notes:

- » Inspect jars for cracks or chips before using.
- » Adjust the recipe for fish quantity and canner size.
- » Allow enough time for the entire canning process.
- » Inspect canned fish before using; when in doubt, discard it.
- » Allocate time for preparation, pressurizing, canning, and depressurizing.

Note on Canned Salmon:

- » Canned salmon may sometimes contain struvite crystals, which look like glass but are magnesium ammonium phosphate. These crystals, which can't be prevented in home canning, are safe to eat and generally dissolve when heated.

Here is the recommended process time for **trout salmon and blue fish** in a dial-gauge pressure canner.

			CANNER PRESSURE (PSI) AT ALTITUDES OF			
Style of pack	Jar Size	Process Time min	0–2,000 ft.	2,001–4,000 ft.	4,001–6,000 ft.	6,001–8,000 ft.
Raw	Pints	100	11 lb	12 lb	13 lb	14 lb

The following is the recommended process time for **trout salmon and blue fish** in a weighted—gauge pressure canner.

			CANNER PRESSURE (PSI) AT ALTITUDES OF	
Style of Pack	Jar size	Time min	0–1,000 ft.	Above 1,000 ft.

			CANNER PRESSURE (PSI) AT ALTITUDES OF	
Raw	Pints	100	10 lb	15 lb

64. TRADITIONAL OYSTER CANNING

INGREDIENTS:

» Oysters: The quantity depends on their size and the number of pint jars you plan to fill. Typically, 1–1 ½ lb of medium-sized oysters are needed per pint jar.
» Pickling salt: 1 tsp per pint jar

» Water: Enough to cover the oysters in each pint jar, maintaining a 1-inch headspace
» Salt for cleaning: ½ cup per gallon of water for rinsing oysters' meat

INSTRUCTIONS:

1. Chilling and opening: Store live oysters in a cool place until you're ready to can them. Clean their shells, then steam them until they open. After steaming, remove the oyster meat.
2. Cleaning oyster meat: Rinse the oyster meat in fresh water, you can add ½ cup of salt per gallon of water for this rinse.
3. Jarring: Place the drained oyster meat into preheated half-pint or pint jars. Optionally, add ¼ tsp of salt per half-pint or ½ tsp per pint. Fill with boiling water, leaving a 1-inch headspace. Release any trapped air bubbles.
4. Sealing jars: Clean the jar rims using a paper towel moistened with vinegar. Securely adjust the lids on the jars.
5. Pressure canning: Process both half-pint and pint jars in a pressure canner for 75 minutes. Use 10 lb of pressure for a weighted gauge and 11 lb for a dial gauge. Adjust the pressure based on your altitude as per the recommended guidelines.

Here is the recommended process time for **oysters**, in a weighted—gauge pressure canner.

		CANNER PRESSURE (PSI) AT ALTITUDES OF			
Jar Size	Process Time min	0–2,000 ft.	2,001–4,000 ft.	4,001–6,000 ft.	6,001–8,000 ft.
Pints and half-pints	75	11 lb	12 lb	13 lb	14 lb

Here is the recommended process time for **oysters**, in a weighted—gauge pressure canner.

		CANNER PRESSURE (PSI) AT ALTITUDES OF	
Jar size	Time min	0–1,000 ft.	Above 1,000 ft.
Pints or half-pints	75	10 lb	15 lb

65. CANNED TUNA RECIPE

INGREDIENTS:
» Tuna fish 6–8 lb

» Salt (optional)
» Water

Yield: 7–8 pints

INSTRUCTIONS:
1. Tuna preparation options: You can opt to can tuna in its raw state to preserve its natural oils and juices or precook it to reduce the oil's strong flavor.
2. Prepping raw tuna: If slightly frozen, tuna is easier to fillet. You can choose to remove the skin before or after this step. For precooking, start by gutting the fish and rinsing it under cold water. You can bake the tuna at 250°F for 2 ½ to 4 hours, or at 350°F for roughly an hour until it reaches an internal temperature of 165–175°F. Alternatively, steam it for the same duration. Chill the tuna post-cooking to firm up the flesh.
3. Cleaning the tuna: Utilize a sharp knife for skinning and gently scrape off any blood vessels and discolored areas on the meat.
4. Slicing the tuna: Quarter the fish, removing all bones and the bases of fins. Exclude the dark meat to maintain the tuna's light taste.
5. Jar filling: Cut the tuna into jar-sized pieces, estimating about ¾ lb per pint jar. Fill the jars with tuna, ensuring a 1-inch head-space.
6. Packing the jars: For raw packed tuna, avoid adding any liquid. If you're using precooked tuna, you may add vegetable oil or water, still leaving a 1-inch headspace. Adding salt is up to your preference.
7. Sealing: Wipe the jar rims with a paper towel dampened with vinegar to ensure a clean seal, then place the lids on top.
8. Canning: Process the jars in a pressure canner, adhering to the manufacturer's guidelines for time and pressure settings.
9. Storing jars: Once cleaned and labeled with the processing date and contents, store your tuna jars in a cool, dry place.

The following is the recommended process time for tuna, in a weighted—gauge pressure canner.

Jar Size	Process Time min	CANNER PRESSURE (PSI) AT ALTITUDES OF			
		0–2,000 ft.	2,001–4,000 ft.	4,001–6,000 ft.	6,001–8,000 ft.
Pints and half-pints	100	11 lb	12 lb	13 lb	14 lb

The following is the recommended process time for tuna, in a weighted—gauge pressure canner.

Jar size	Time min	CANNER PRESSURE (PSI) AT ALTITUDES OF	
		0–1,000 ft.	Above 1,000 ft.
Pints or half-pints	100	10 lb	15 lb

66. CLASSIC SHRIMP CANNING

INGREDIENTS:

» 2 gallons water
» 2 cups salt for brine,

» 4 tbsp salt for packing
» 2 cups vinegar
» 5 lb shrimp

INSTRUCTIONS:

1. Brine preparation: In a large pot, mix water, vinegar, and 2 cups of salt to create a flavor brine.
2. Shrimp preparation: As soon as you catch the shrimp, remove their heads and keep them chilled until you're ready to can. Thoroughly wash and then drain the shrimp.
3. Cooking: Boil the shrimp for 8–10 minutes in an acidic brine mixture (salt and vinegar in water). After boiling, rinse them in cold water and drain again.
4. Peeling: Remove the shells from the cooked shrimp.

PRESSURE CANNING:

1. Packing jars: Place the peeled shrimp into preheated half-pint or pint jars, leaving 1 inch of headspace. For a less salty option, use boiling water instead of brine.
2. Adding brine: Ladle hot brine or boiling water over the shrimp, ensuring a 1-inch headspace. Remove air bubbles.
3. Sealing jars: Wipe jar rims with vinegar-dampened cloth. Secure lids and rings.
4. Canning process: Fill the pressure canner with hot water as recommended. Place the filled jars inside, secure the lid, and set the canner on high heat to bring it to a boil.
5. Venting: Allow the canner to vent steam for 10 minutes. Then, close the vent and adjust the heat to reach the required pressure: 11 PSI for a dial gauge or 10 PSI for a weighted gauge, modifying as necessary for your altitude.
6. Processing time: Process both pint and half-pint jars for 45 minutes.
7. Cooling down: After the processing time, turn off the heat and let the pressure return to zero naturally. This may take 30 minutes or longer. Once the pressure is zero, carefully open the canner lid, avoiding the steam.
8. Resting the jars: Let the jars sit in the canner for an additional 10 minutes before removing them.
9. Cooling the jars: Place the jars on a cutting board and leave them undisturbed to cool for at least 8–12 hours.
10. Finishing steps: After cooling, check the seals, then remove the rings, and wash the jars in warm, soapy water. Label each jar with the product name and the date of storage. Finally, store the jars in a cool, dark place, like a pantry or cellar.

Notes:

- Flavoring: Season the shrimp with salt, pepper, garlic, or other spices for enhanced flavor.
- Spoilage check: Regularly check jars for spoilage indicators like broken seals or off smells. Discard if necessary.

Here is the recommended process time for **shrimp**, in dial-gauge pressure canner.

Style of pack	Jar size	Process Time min	CANNER PRESSURE (PSI) AT ALTITUDES OF			
			0–2,000 ft.	2,001–4,000 ft.	4,001–6,000 ft.	6,001–8,000 ft.
Hot	Half-pints or pints	45	11 lb	12 lb	13 lb	14 lb

Here is the recommended process time for **shrimp,** in a weighted—gauge pressure canner.

Style of Pack	Jar size	Time min	CANNER PRESSURE (PSI) AT ALTITUDES OF	
			0–1,000 ft.	Above 1,000 ft.
Hot	Half-pints or pints	45	10 lb	15 lb

Checking Canned Seafood:

- Visual inspection: Examine each jar before use. Check for external streaks, cloudy liquid inside, air bubbles, or unnatural colors.
- Opening the jar: Be cautious of spurting liquids or mold growth on the food or under the lid. Smell for off odors and never taste food from jars that seem spoiled or unsealed.

Disposal of Spoiled Food:

- Sealed jars: Label sealed, suspect jars as poison and dispose of them in a heavy-duty garbage bag in your trash or at a landfill.
- Unsealed or leaking jars: Detoxify these jars before disposal.

Detoxification Process:

- Wear gloves and handle the suspect food carefully.
- Remove lids and place jars and lids in a large pot.
- Cover jars with water, ensuring they are submerged by 1 inch. Boil for 30 minutes.
- Dispose of the containers, lids, and contents after cooling.
- Clean surfaces with a chlorine bleach solution (1 part unscented bleach to 5 parts water), let it sit for 30 minutes, then clean and rinse thoroughly. Discard gloves after cleaning.

If No Spoilage is Detected:

- To ensure safety, heat canned fish before consumption. Boil on a stovetop for 10 minutes or heat in the oven to avoid texture changes.

CHAPTER 11
FERMENTING RECIPES

"Fermented food enhances the flavor, providing a unique, probiotic-rich profile that promotes your well-being. An excellent choice as a nutritious snack to elevate your health and your dishes."

Guidelines for Fermentation

Ensuring adherence to exemplary manufacturing practices is crucial throughout the fermentation process. These practices emphasize the importance of cleanliness and thorough preparation to guarantee the safety and quality of fermented products.

1. **Hygiene and Preparation:**
   - Prioritize the cleanliness of fresh produce, hands, utensils, and all containers by washing them thoroughly.
   - Choose vegetables that are ripe, free from damage, and of uniform size for consistency.

2. **Setting Up the Fermentation Environment:**
   - Secure the fermentation vessel in place to avoid any disturbances during the process.
   - Avoid the practice of backslapping to maintain cultural integrity.

3. **Managing the Fermentation Process:**
   - Create an anaerobic (oxygen-free) environment by ensuring the ferment is completely submerged under liquid and the container is sealed properly.
   - Any product showing signs of discoloration (pink or dark) should be discarded to prevent the risk of spoilage.

4. **Monitoring and Documentation:**
   - Keep a detailed log of temperature and pH levels throughout the fermentation to monitor the process accurately.
   - Ensure all equipment is calibrated correctly and maintain documentation of such calibrations.
   - Store all records for a minimum of two years, although requirements may vary depending on the product.

5. **Storage of Fermented Products:**
   - Store the finished fermented products in a refrigerator, maintaining a temperature below 40°F to preserve freshness and prevent spoilage.

Fermentation Processes Guidelines (Optimal salt Level)

FOOD	OPTIMAL SALT LEVEL	OPTIMAL TEMPERATURE RANGE	TIME RANGE FOR FERMENTATION COMPLETION
Cucumbers	5–8% (brine)	59–89,6°F	
Cabbage	2,25% (by weight of cabbage)	60–70°F 70–75°F	* 5–6 weeks * 3–4 weeks
Kimchi	4–6% (brine or by weight)	50–64°F	* 5–20 days
Fruit	2–3% (brine or by weight)	50–59°F	2–6 weeks

* Fermentation is complete when the product reaches a below 4,6

Kombucha production guidelines (Starter Culture)

FOOD	STARTER CULTURE	OPTIMAL TEMPERATURE RANGE	TIME RANGE FOR FERMENTATION COMPLETION
Kombucha	Bring to a boil before adding	75–85°F	12 days minimum

Guidelines for Kombucha production:

1. **Starter Culture Preparation:**
    - If you're using a dehydrated starter culture like (SCOBY) follow the manufacturer's instructions, often involving vinegar.

2. **Temperature and Fermentation Time:**
    - Adjust fermentation for colder temperatures by extending the time to compensate for reduced microbial activity.

3. **Ph Level Control:**
    - Test the pH level with guidance from a Process Authority.

4. **Alcohol Content Verification:**
    - Confirm a maximum alcohol content of 0.5% by volume through laboratory testing.

5. **Bottling Procedure:**
    - Use sterile bottles if bottling the product.

6. **Storage and Labeling:**
    - After fermentation, refrigerate the product (below 40°F).
    - Label the product as "keep refrigerated."

Storage Methods

FOOD	REFRIGERATION	CANNING	FREEZER
Kombucha	X		
Fermented Pickles	X	X Raw pack: Pints 15 minutes Quarts 20 minutes	
Kimchi	X		
Sauerkraut	X	X Raw pack: Pints 25 Quarts 30 minutes Hot pack: Pints 15 Quarts 20 minutes	X

Storage and Handling of Fermented Products

- When storing fermented products, ensure your hands are clean and use clean utensils for handling and transferring to maintain food safety.
- Remember, fermentation is not a sterilization method. Proper storage is vital for food safety.

- Refrigeration is important: It's highly recommended to refrigerate fermented products, whether through canning or freezing, depending on the specific product.
- Maintaining brine: To prevent softening during storage, ensure that the vegetables remain fully submerged in the brine.
- Kombucha: Store in the refrigerator to halt or slow alcohol production.
- Fermented Pickles: Store in the refrigerator or can them by boiling for longer preservation (15 minutes for pints and 20 minutes for quarts).
- Kimchi: Keep it in the fridge for storage.
- Sauerkraut: It can be stored in the fermentation vessel in a cool, dark area for up to three months, keeping the sauerkraut submerged in the brine. Alternatively, refrigerate, freeze (8–12 months), or process in a boiling water bath canner for shelf storage as in the table.

Preparation and Fermentation; Step-by-Step Recipes

Cleaning and Preparation
- Thoroughly clean all utensils, the glass jar, and the canning jar. Wash your hands with soap.

Preparing the Vegetables
- Use fresh, firm, and preferably organic vegetables.
- Wash the vegetables thoroughly, removing wilted or damaged parts.
- Cut the vegetables into pieces or strips of the desired size.

Chopping and Salting
- In a large bowl, combine the cut vegetables with salt.
- Massage and press the vegetables with salt to release their juice. This process may take 5 to 10 minutes.

Fermentation Container
- Use a fermentation container or a food-grade glass or plastic container with an airtight seal.
- Pack the salted vegetables tightly into the container, pressing them down with a pestle or your hands.

Weighting the Vegetables
- Use a weight or a bag filled with brine to keep the vegetables submerged in their juice.
- Cover the container with a clean cloth to allow air circulation and secure it to prevent the entry of debris or insects, ensuring a proper and undisturbed fermentation process.

Fermentation Conditions
- Vegetable fermentation can vary depending on the type and temperature. Please follow the process guidelines in the table above.
- Maintain a temperature between 65–75°C for optimal fermentation, while lower temperatures may extend the process.
- Avoid temperatures exceeding 75°C, as they can negatively impact fermentation.

Monitoring and Adjusting

- Taste the vegetables after a few days and regularly press them for additional juice release.
- If the vegetables are not fully covered within a day, add a saltwater solution
- (1 tsp of salt in 1 cup of water).
- During fermentation, watch for the presence of bubbles, foam, or molds. Remove any molds if they appear.

Fermentation Duration

- The fermentation duration can vary depending on the type of vegetables and personal preferences. Typically, fermentation lasts from a few days to several weeks.
- Taste the vegetables during the process and stop fermentation once the desired flavor is achieved.

Storage and Use

- Once fermentation is complete, store the fermented vegetables in clean, airtight containers in the refrigerator to keep them for several weeks or months, depending on the product.

Guide to Calculating Salt for Fermentation

When fermenting vegetables, the right amount of salt is crucial. You'll need a 2% to 3% salt solution, based on the total weight of the ingredients (including water). Here's a step-by-step guide, with conversions to U.S. measurements for your convenience.

Steps for Salt Calculation

1. Weigh the jar: Start by weighing your empty fermentation jar and note the weight.
1. Add ingredients: Fill the jar with vegetables, spices, and enough water to cover everything.
2. Weigh again: Weigh the filled jar to determine the total weight of the jar plus its contents.
3. Calculate ingredients' weight: Subtract the weight of the empty jar from the total weight to find the weight of the vegetables and water combined.
4. Determine salt amount: Calculate 2%–3% of the total weight (from step 4) to get the amount of salt needed. For accuracy, use a digital scale.
5. Add salt: Mix the calculated amount of salt directly into the jar, ensuring it's well distributed.
6. Ferment: Seal the jar and let the fermentation process begin.

Examples

For 2.2 lb (1 kg) of vegetables, you need 3 ½–5 ¼ tsp (20–30 gr) of salt.

- 2% Solution: 20 grams ≈ 3 ½ tsp
- 3% Solution: 30 grams ≈ 5 ¼ tsp

Using the right amount of salt is crucial for the success of fermentation. It not only enhances the flavor but also ensures the safety and preservation of the vegetables. Precision in measuring salt is key to maintaining the quality of your fermented products. The correct salt concentration helps prevent harmful bacteria, allowing only beneficial fermentation to occur.

This makes your fermented foods safe to eat and delicious. For the most accurate measurements, it's recommended to use the metric system, with grams for salt and milliliters for liquid. This approach is more precise than the imperial system and ensures the proper salt proportions for effective fermentation.

This table offers an easy guide to sauerkraut's storage and fermentation options, detailing timeframes and key tips for each method.

STORAGE/ FERMENTATION CONDITION	DURATION	NOTES
Unopened refrigerated storage	Lasts up to 2 years	Keep a cabbage leaf on top and seal with a standard lid.
Opened refrigerated storage	Good for 1–3 months	Consume regularly; keep submerged in brine.
Storage without refrigeration	Keep at temperatures below 50°F (10°C) ideally in a root cellar	If unavailable, opt for refrigeration.
Counter fermentation (50–60°F or 10–17°C)	Takes about 8–12 weeks	After completion, the transfer to the refrigerator.
Counter Fermentation (70–75°F or 21–24°C)	Duration is 4–6 weeks	Refrigerate post-fermentation.
Counter Fermentation (80–89°F or 27–32°C)	Duration is 2–4 weeks	Afterward, store in the refrigerator.
Counter Fermentation (Above 90°F or 33°C)	Complete within 3–7 days	Refrigerate subsequently.

Sauerkraut

"Easy Homemade Sauerkraut in 4 Steps"

- Shred cabbage, mix with salt, and knead until juicy.
- Pack into a jar, using a weigh to submerge.
- Let natural bacteria turn sugars into acid, stopping bad bacteria.
- Ferment 3–10 days, then enjoy your sauerkraut.Inizio modulo

67. CLASSIC CABBAGE SAUERKRAUT

INGREDIENTS:

- » 3 lb green or red cabbage (approximately 1 medium head)
- » 1 ½ tbsp pickling or sea salt
- » 1 tbsp caraway seeds (optional, for flavor)
- » Begin sauerkraut preparation within 24–48 hours after harvest.

INSTRUCTIONS:

1. Start by thoroughly cleaning all utensils and containers to create an optimal environment for beneficial bacteria during fermentation. Wash the mason jar, jelly jar, and your hands.
2. Prepare the cabbage by removing any wilted outer leaves. Cut the cabbage into quarters, remove the core, and slice each quarter into thin ribbons.
3. Combine the sliced cabbage with the salt in a large bowl. Massage and squeeze the cabbage to work the salt in. The cabbage will gradually become more pliable and release its water, resembling coleslaw. This will take 5 to 10 minutes. If you want to flavor the sauerkraut with caraway seeds, stir them in now.
4. Pack the salted cabbage into a canning jar, pressing it down with your fist. Place an outer cabbage leaf on top for better submersion.
5. Use a fermentation weight to press the cabbage down and keep it submerged in its liquid.
6. Cover the jar with a cloth and secure it, allowing air to circulate while preventing dust or insects from entering.
7. If the cabbage isn't fully covered by liquid after 24 hours, dissolve a tsp of salt in a cup of water and add enough to submerge the cabbage.
8. Ferment the cabbage for 3 to 10 days at a cool room temperature (65°F to 75°F), checking and pressing it daily.

9. Taste the sauerkraut after 3 days and refrigerate once it reaches your desired flavor. It can continue fermenting for up to 10 days or longer if preferred.
10. During fermentation, look for signs like bubbles, foam, or white scum, which indicate a healthy fermentation process. Skim off any mold if it appears.
11. After complete fermentation, sauerkraut can be stored in the refrigerator for several months, and often much longer, as long as it maintains its good taste and smell. If you wish to store it for an extended period, you can preserve it by using the hot pack or raw method.

Hot pack: Slowly bring the sauerkraut and liquid to a boil in a large pot, stirring often. Remove from the heat and fill jars fairly firmly with kraut and liquid, leaving a ½-inch headspace. Wipe the edges of the jar clean. Adjust the lids. Process 10 minutes per pint; and 15 minutes per quart in a boiling water bath.

Raw pack: Fill jars well with kraut and liquid, leaving ½ inch headspace. Clean the edges of the jar. Adjust lids. Process pints for 20 minutes, and quarts for 25 minutes in a boiling water bath.

Notes:

- You can use different types of cabbage to make sauerkraut, such as red cabbage or Napa cabbage, for variations in flavor and color.
- Canning sauerkraut is possible for longer storage but will kill the beneficial bacteria from fermentation.
- Adjust quantities of cabbage and salt for larger or smaller batches, maintaining the same ratio.
- Store sauerkraut at a cool room temperature to avoid undesirable texture or spoilage. Cold temperatures are acceptable, but fermentation will proceed more slowly.

68. HOMEMADE SAUERKRAUT MADE EASY

INGREDIENTS:

- » 1 head green or red cabbage
- » 2 tsp salt
- » Glass mason jars with screw-on lids

OPTIONAL INGREDIENTS FOR FLAVOR:

- » Fresh ginger root knob (peeled and grated)
- » 1 garlic clove peeled
- » Fennel or caraway seeds
- » 1 tsp cinnamon

INSTRUCTIONS:

1. Start by removing and composting the outer leaves of the cabbage. Rinse the remaining cabbage thoroughly and chop it into ¼-inch thick strips (you can go thinner if you prefer).
2. Place all the chopped cabbage in a large mixing bowl and evenly sprinkle the salt over it. Use clean hands to knead and massage the salt into the cabbage. If you like, you can add any of the optional spices and flavors mentioned in the list, or use your favorites.
3. Pack the salted cabbage tightly into glass mason jars. Depending on the jar size, you might fill one or more. Leave about an inch of space between the cabbage and the jar's rim to allow cabbage juice to cover the cabbage during fermentation.
4. To ensure there are no air pockets, press the cabbage down firmly using a tamper (you can use one from a blender). It's essential to submerge even the top strips in the cabbage juice.
5. Place the weight for fermentation in the jar and loosely cover the jars with lids—don't screw them on tightly. This allows beneficial bacteria to access the air they need for fermentation.
6. Every day, press down on the cabbage with a tamper to eliminate any air pockets below the fill line. The sauerkraut will be ready in about four weeks, but the timing can vary based on your local climate.
7. Taste the sauerkraut to determine the flavor and acidity level you prefer. Once you're satisfied, you can screw the lids on and refrigerate the sauerkraut to stop the fermentation process.

69. BEET-INFUSED SAUERKRAUT

INGREDIENTS:

- » ¾ lb red cabbage
- » 1 medium beet, grated
- » 1-pound green cabbage
- » 1 cup water
- » 1 ½ tsp sea salt
- » 1 tbsp anise seed

Yields: About 3–4 pints

INSTRUCTIONS:

Mix all ingredients in a large bowl, and continue the process following the directions for Classic Cabbage Sauerkraut.

70. BEETROOT AND GINGER SAUERKRAUT

INGREDIENTS:

- » 1 lb thinly sliced red cabbage
- » ¼ cup finely grated organic ginger
- » ½ lb red beets, washed and grated
- » 1–½ tbsp sea salt
- » 1 tsp dill or fennel seed

INSTRUCTIONS:

1. Combine the three mixtures with the other ingredients in a large bowl, and continue the process following the directions for Classic Cabbage Sauerkraut.

71. SAUERKRAUT WITH APPLE

» **Ingredients:**
» 1 medium cabbage (finely shredded). Keep some outer leaves aside.
» 2 sour and firm apples (peeled, cored, and chopped)
» 1 tsp freshly ginger root (grated)
» 1 tsp sea salt

Yields: About 3 pints

INSTRUCTIONS:
Combine the two mixtures with the other ingredients in a large bowl, and continue the process following the directions for Classic Cabbage Sauerkraut.

72. CARROT AND SAUERKRAUT MIX

INGREDIENTS:

» 1 small cabbage (approximately 2 lb) finely shredded. Keep some outer leaves aside.

» 1 large carrot
» 1 tbsp sea salt
» 2 tsp dill or fennel seeds (grind the seeds lightly)

INSTRUCTIONS:
1. Follow the instructions for Classic Cabbage Sauerkraut. Prepare the carrot using the wider holes of a grater. Mix it with the ground seeds, and add to the cabbage with salt. Proceed with the sauerkraut pounding process.

73. SAUERKRAUT WITH ORANGE FLAVOR

» **Ingredients:**
» 1 small cabbage (2 lb) finely shredded
» 1 orange with edible peel

» 1 tbsp sea salt
» A sprig thyme

INSTRUCTIONS:
1. After massaging the cabbage with salt and extracting water, add orange slices and thyme. Continue Follow the instructions for Classic Cabbage Sauerkraut.

74. FERMENTED TANGY COLESLAW

» **Ingredients:**
» 1 ½ lb cabbage
» ½ small daikon radish
» ½ onion
» 2 celery ribs
» 1 carrot
» 1 ½ parsley sprigs
» 2 tbsp ginger, fresh turmeric
» 1 garlic head
» 1–2 tbsp sea salt

INSTRUCTIONS:
1. Chop or grate the vegetables evenly, mix with salt, and blend well with your hands. Follow the Classic Cabbage Sauerkraut preparation instructions.

75. TURMERIC-GINGER PINEAPPLE SAUERKRAUT

» **Ingredients:**
» 3 lb shredded cabbage
» 1 ¼ lb diced pineapple
» 2 tbsp freshly grated ginger
» 2 tbsp sea salt
» 1 tbsp turmeric powder
» A pinch ground black pepper (optional)
» 8 mint leaves, roughly chopped

INSTRUCTIONS:
1. After blending the salt into the cabbage, kneading and squeezing it to soften and release its liquid, you can then introduce additional ingredients such as pineapple, ginger, and any other chosen flavorings. Continue by following the steps outlined for Classic Cabbage Sauerkraut.

76. FERMENTED DILL CUCUMBER PICKLES

INGREDIENTS:

- » 1 lb Kirby cucumbers (aim for small, uniform sizes)
- » 1 grape leaf
- » 3 bay leaves
- » 1 tsp black peppercorns
- » 2 garlic cloves, sliced
- » 1 dill flower or (2 tsp dill seeds)
- » 1 ½ tsp coriander seeds

BRINE:

- » To create a 3% brine solution, maintain this consistent salt-to-water ratio, adjusting the quantity as needed depending on your fermentation vessel's size:
- » Use 1 level tbsp of fine-grain salt for every quart (950ml) of water.

INSTRUCTIONS:

1. Wash cucumbers, paying extra attention to scrubbing the blossom ends to remove pectic enzymes. Soak them in an ice water bath for at least 1 hour while you prepare other ingredients.
2. In a clean 1-quart mason jar, layer grape leaf, bay leaf, garlic cloves, and dill flower or seeds. Grape leaves provide tannins that preserve cucumber crispness. If not available, alternatives include oak, sour cherry, or horseradish leaves, an extra bay leaf, or a pinch of green or black tea.
3. Top off the jar with any remaining dill, but make sure to leave a 2–3 headspace at the top for the weight.
4. Place the fermentation weight into the jar, and then pour the brine over the cucumbers.
5. Place a loosely fitted lid on the jar. A loose lid allows fermentation gases to escape without needing to burp the jar.
6. Leave the container on the counter, away from direct sunlight, for 5 to 8 days for fermentation. Keep in mind that a longer fermentation period can result in softer cucumbers.

DURING FERMENTATION:

- » While the fermentation is ongoing, keep an eye out for these positive indicators:
- » You should notice bubbles rising in the jar when you gently tap or swirl it.
- » The brine may appear cloudy, which is perfectly normal.
- » The cucumber color may transition from a vibrant green to a more subdued hue.
- » As the cucumbers ferment, they might shrink and settle lower in the jar due to moisture loss.
- » It's common for bubbles or foam to form on the surface of the brine.
- » You may see cloudy sediment at the bottom of the jar and occasionally on the pickles themselves. These are all healthy signs of the fermentation process.
- » After fermentation, remove the fermenting weight and clear any kahm yeast that may have developed.

STORAGE:

- » Once fermentation is complete, store the vegetables in clean airtight containers in the refrigerator for several months.
- » Seal the jar with a mason jar lid and ring, and store it in the refrigerator for long-term preservation.

77. GINGERED CARROT LACTO-FERMENTED

- » **Ingredients:**
- » 1 lb carrots (about 4 large ones)
- » A handful fresh dill (optional)
- » ¼ tsp red chili flakes (optional)
- » 3–4 whole peeled garlic cloves
- » 3–5 slices ginger
- » Salt and water for the brine (3 tbsp sea salt per 2 pints of water)

Yield: About 2 pints

INSTRUCTIONS:

1. Start by thoroughly washing and peeling the carrots. Cut them diagonally into broad slices, about a quarter-inch thick, making sure they are short enough to fit under a fermentation weight in the jar.
2. In the fermentation jar, layer the sliced carrots with dill, ginger slices, and garlic cloves, leaving some free space at the top of the jar.
3. Slowly pour the brine over the carrots, ensuring they are fully submerged.
4. Use a tamper, chopstick, or your clean fingers to press the carrots down below the surface of the brine.
5. Insert a fermentation weight into the jar to keep everything submerged.
6. Cover the jar with a lid that is fitted loosely; this setup allows gases produced during fermentation to escape without the need to manually "burp" the jar.
7. Set the jar on a towel or plate to catch any overflow of brine that may occur.
8. Let the carrots ferment at a room temperature between 70–80°F (20–27°C) for a period ranging from 8 to 21 days, depending on your taste preferences and the room's temperature.
9. Once fermentation is complete, remove the weight, skim off any kahm yeast that may have formed, tightly seal the jar, and refrigerate. The fermented carrots can be enjoyed for several months.

78. LACTO-FERMENTED TURNIPS AND BEETS

INGREDIENTS:

- » 3 medium turnips
- » 1 small beet
- » 1 grape leaf (optional)
- » 1–2 garlic cloves
- » 2 bay leaves
- » Brine: 2 tsp sea salt and 2 cups water

Yield: 2–3 pints

INSTRUCTIONS:

1. Start by dissolving the salt in water within a half-liter jar, stirring until fully dissolved.
2. Peel the turnips and beet, trimming off the stem and root ends. Slice them into half-inch thick sticks.
3. Thinly slice the garlic cloves. Place these slices at the bottom of a 1-quart or 2-pint glass jar, along with the bay leaves. Then, layer in the turnip, and beet sticks up to the neck of the jar.
4. Compress the vegetables down to ensure they're snugly packed, but stop filling when you're an inch from the top of the jar.
5. If using, place a grape leaf over the top to help the turnips and beets stay crisp (alternatively, black tea leaves or oak leaves can be used). This helps keep the vegetables submerged in the brine.
6. Since turnips may float, employ a weight to keep them beneath the brine surface, ensuring the jar is filled with brine but leaving some headspace.
7. Seal the jar with a fermentation-friendly lid and store it in a cool, dark location for 2 to 4 weeks, checking daily.
8. Taste the fermentation after 3 days to check for desired sourness.
9. Once satisfied with the fermentation level, tightly seal the jar and refrigerate. Enjoy your tangy fermented turnips and beets as a crisp, flavorful addition to meals

79. ONION LACTO-FERMENTED

INGREDIENTS:

» 1-pound onion (red, yellow, or a mix)
» 1 tsp spices (choose from cumin, coriander, black pepper, fenugreek
» Brine: (5%) 1 cup water 2,5 tsp sea salt

Yield: about 1–2 pints

INSTRUCTIONS:

1. Begin by mixing the sliced onions with the salt in a large bowl. Massage the onions with your hands until they start releasing their natural juices and soften.
2. Firmly pack the salted onions into a fermentation jar, making sure to include the released juices.
3. Add a fermentation weight over the onions. At first, the onions might not be fully covered by their liquid. Pour in just enough of the prepared brine to submerge the onions completely beneath the weight.
4. Seal the jar with a fermentation-friendly lid and set it in a room-temperature location away from direct sunlight for the fermentation process.
5. After 24 hours, check if the onions have expelled additional liquid. Top up with a little water, if necessary, to ensure the onions remain submerged, then reseal with the lid and airlock. Continue to ferment the mixture at room temperature, avoiding sunlight, for a period of 7 to 10 days.
6. Once the fermentation period is complete, move the fermented onions to storage jars and refrigerate. These lacto-fermented onions will keep well in the refrigerator for up to two months.

80. FERMENTED RADISH RECIPE

Radishes are not only a visually appealing and tasty addition to any dish but are also packed with health benefits. Their unique flavor, attributed to mustard oils, not only adds zest but also supports liver health and may have anti-diabetic benefits according to recent studies.

INGREDIENTS:

» 1 bunch radishes
» 1 ½ tsp sea salt mixed with 1 cup water to create a 3% salt brine
» 1 tsp mustard seeds
» 1–2 stalks Thai basil (horapha)
» Optional: Experiment with additional herbs and spices such as garlic, dill, thyme, sage, scallions, peppercorns, chili rings, or onion slices

Yield: Approximately 1–2 pints

INSTRUCTIONS:

1. Begin by thoroughly cleaning the radishes and trimming off their tops. Remember, the greens are edible and versatile in culinary uses (see below for ideas).
2. Prepare a 3% salt brine by dissolving 1 ½ tsp of salt in 1 cup of water.
3. At the bottom of your fermentation container, place your chosen herbs and spices. Add the radishes next, and pour the prepared brine over them to cover.
4. To ensure a successful fermentation, the radishes and spices must remain submerged in the brine. Fermentation weights can help maintain everything below the surface.
5. Start the fermentation process at room temperature, usually in a warm kitchen area, for a minimum of 3 days. The ideal flavor is often reached after 4–5 days, but taste testing during fermentation will help you find your perfect balance of acidity. Always use clean utensils to taste or remove radishes. Once the desired taste is achieved, transfer the jar to the refrigerator to slow further fermentation.

Notes:

- Embracing a zero-waste approach in the kitchen is rewarding. Radish greens, frequently discarded, are surprisingly flavorful and nutritious. They can be sautéed with onions, blended into a creamy soup, or turned into a vibrant pesto with nuts or seeds and quality oil, offering a unique way to utilize the entire plant.

81. GARLIC FERMENTED IN HONEY

INGREDIENTS:

» 1 cup garlic cloves
» 1 cup (or more) unpasteurized honey, enough to fully cover the garlic
» 1 tsp cloves

Yield: About 1 pint

INSTRUCTIONS:

1. Start by peeling the garlic cloves. Discard any that appear damaged or discolored. For larger cloves, consider cutting them into halves or quarters to ensure even fermentation.
2. In a clean jar, place both the garlic cloves and a tsp of cloves, filling it to about half full.
3. Carefully pour the unpasteurized honey over the garlic until they are completely submerged, leaving around a quarter of the jar's space empty to allow for expansion and prevent overflow.
4. Place the jar on a plate to catch any overflow and securely seal the jar.
5. Let the jar sit at room temperature for several weeks. You'll notice the honey will become more liquid-like, turning syrupy, and it's normal for the garlic to darken in color.
6. During the first week, open the jar daily to release any accumulated gases, then give the jar a gentle shake to redistribute the contents.
7. Continue to stir the mixture once a week after the first week, keeping the jar otherwise closed. The honey will further liquefy, and the garlic may darken even more. For safety, particularly to guard against botulism, consider using a pH test strip to ensure the pH is below 4.6, given that honey's natural pH hovers around 3.9.
8. The honey-fermented garlic can be consumed after one month, but letting it age for longer periods, such as 2, 6, or even 12 months, will further develop its flavor and enhance its qualities.

82. LEMON LACTO-FERMENTED

INGREDIENTS:

» 12 lemons
» 6 tsp salt
» 3 bay leaves
» 2 cinnamon sticks
» 6 cloves
» 3 stars anises
» Enough water to cover the lemons

Yield: about 3 Pints

INSTRUCTIONS:

1. Begin by thoroughly washing the lemons, especially if they're not organic. It's best to use warm water, ensuring it's comfortable to touch.
2. Slice off the ends of each lemon and quarter them, taking care to remove any seeds encountered.
3. Mix the lemon quarters with salt in a bowl. Use your hands to gently crush the lemons with the salt to combine them well and start releasing their juices.
4. Tightly pack the salted lemon pieces into a clean jar. Between layers, add the bay leaves, cinnamon sticks, cloves, and star anises for flavor infusion.
5. Pour water over the packed lemons and spices, maintaining a 2 cm gap below the jar's lip. Place a fermentation weight over the lemons to ensure they stay fully submerged.
6. Close the jar securely and set aside at room temperature to ferment for 30 days, allowing the lemons to pickle and develop flavor.

Notes:

• The lemons can continue to ferment at room temperature for up to a year, enhancing their flavor complexity over time.

• After initially opening the jar, it should be stored in the refrigerator. Use these aromatic preserved lemons to elevate the taste of your meals whenever desired!

83. CHERRY TOMATOES FERMENTED

INGREDIENTS:

»   2 ½ lb cherry tomatoes
»   4 cups water
»   4 ½ springs fresh dill or basil

»   2 tbsp sea salt
»   4–5 garlic cloves, sliced
»   1 ½ tsp whole black peppercorn
»   1 ½ tbsp mustard seeds

Yield: About 5 pints

INSTRUCTIONS:

1.   Dissolve the sea salt in water by stirring them together until fully mixed.
2.   Place the sliced garlic, mustard seeds, black peppercorns, and fresh dill or basil at the bottom of a large glass jar.
3.   Carefully add the cherry tomatoes over the layer of spices and herbs in the jar.
4.   Gently pour the saltwater solution over the cherry tomatoes, making sure they are entirely submerged.
5.   Close the jar with its lid and set it to ferment in a dark, cool place for about 7 days. You'll notice fermentation activity as bubbles start to form in the jar. It's important to open the jar once a day to release any built-up gas.
6.   After 5 to 7 days, sample the cherry tomatoes to gauge their fermentation progress. They will become softer and more flavorful over time. If desired, allow them to ferment for a few additional days until they meet your preference for flavor and texture.
7.   Once the cherry tomatoes have fermented to your liking, transfer them with the brine to sealed glass jars and refrigerate.

Notes:

•   The fermentation duration can vary depending on the thickness of the tomato skins. Avoid over-fermenting to prevent the tomatoes from becoming too soft or breaking apart. They are ideally fermented when soft yet still hold their shape.

84. RED CABBAGE AND MANGO FERMENTATION

INGREDIENTS:

» 3 1/3 lb (about 1 ½ kg) large-head red cabbage
» sea salt
» Filtered water
» 1 ripe mango

INSTRUCTIONS:

1. Begin by finely shredding or chopping the red cabbage.
2. Calculate 2% of the total weight of the cabbage and mango combined to determine the amount of salt needed. For every 2 ¼ lb (1 kg) of the mixture, use approximately 0.7 ounce (20g) of sea salt.
3. In a large bowl, massage the salt into the cabbage until it starts to release its natural juices.
4. Peel and chop the mango into small pieces, then fold it into the cabbage mixture.
5. Transfer the cabbage and mango blend into a Mason jar or a similar fermentation vessel. Press down the mixture to ensure it is fully submerged in its juice, eliminating any air pockets. Using fermentation weights can help keep everything below the liquid surface.
6. Allow for about 2 inches of headspace at the top of the jar to accommodate expansion and prevent overflow during the fermentation process.
7. Securely seal the jar and mark it with the contents and the date of preparation.
8. Let the jar sit at room temperature for 3–5 days to kick-start the fermentation process.
9. After this initial period, transfer the jar to a cooler location, such as a refrigerator, to slow down the fermentation and prevent it from becoming too acidic.
10. The fermented red cabbage and mango should be ready to enjoy after 2–3 weeks.
11. Keep the jar refrigerated, where it can be stored for several months.

Notes:

• This unique combination of red cabbage and mango offers a delightful twist on traditional ferments. The mango adds a sweet contrast to the savory cabbage, creating a fermented dish that's both refreshing and complex in flavor. Give this recipe a try for an unexpected but delicious addition to your fermentation repertoire.

85. PLUMS LACTO-FERMENTED

INGREDIENTS:

» About 14 ounces (400 gr) plums, or enough to fill your jar
» 2 tsp (10 gr) sea salt
» 3–4 cardamom pods
» Lactic acid bacteria culture
» Water as needed

INSTRUCTIONS:

1. If desired, quarter the plums to remove the pits, though you can also ferment them whole.
2. In a mixing bowl, thoroughly combine the plums with sea salt.
3. Allow the salted plums to rest for about 30 minutes, which helps to start drawing out their natural juices.
4. Transfer the salted plums into a fermentation jar, adding the cardamom pods to them.
5. Introduce a source of lactic acid bacteria into the jar to initiate the fermentation process. If using a fermentation weight, place it over the plums to keep them submerged, then add just enough water to cover the plums entirely.
6. Tightly seal the jar with its lid.
7. Begin the fermentation process at room temperature. For a mildly sweet and sour flavor, ferment for about one week. If you prefer a more pronounced tanginess, let the fermentation extend to a month.
8. Once fermentation has reached your desired level of tanginess, remove any weights used and transfer the jar to the refrigerator for storage.

OPTIONS FOR LACTIC ACID BACTERIA SOURCES:

- A commercial lactic acid bacteria starter packet, specifically designed for fruit fermentations.
- A tbsp of brine from another successful lacto-fermentation project.
- A tbsp of whey, extracted from natural yogurt or kefir, containing live cultures.

Notes:

- The selection of the lactic acid bacteria source is a key element in ensuring successful and safe fruit fermentation. Each option provides a different set of microorganisms that can influence the flavor and progression of the fermentation.

86. FERMENTED MIXED BERRIES

» **Ingredients:**
» 4 cups assorted berries (such as blueberries, raspberries, strawberries, and blackberries)

» 4 tbsp honey
» 1 packet starter culture (or a suitable alternative like whey)
» ½ tsp fine sea salt

Yield: About 2 pints/ 1-quart jar

INSTRUCTIONS:

1. Pack the berries tightly into 2 pint-sized jars or a single quart-sized jar, using clean hands or a wooden spoon for firm packing.
2. In a separate container, mix the starter culture with a small amount of water (a few tbsp should suffice), honey, and sea salt until well combined.
3. Carefully pour the mixture over the berries in the jar, ensuring even coverage. Then, fill the jar with filtered water, leaving about 2–3 inches of headspace at the top.
4. Use your fist or a wooden spoon to press down on the berries, eliminating any air pockets. If necessary, add more water to ensure all berries are fully submerged.
5. To keep the berries submerged beneath the liquid, consider using a fermentation weight.
6. Close the jar with its lid and let it sit at room temperature for 1–2 days for initial fermentation.
7. After 1–2 days, move the jar to the refrigerator. The fermented berries are best used within 1–2 months.

FERMENTATION TIP:

- Utilizing a starter culture for fermenting quick-ferment items like fruit chutneys or condiments provides an effective jumpstart to the process. You can find commercial starter cultures in stores, but whey from yogurt or brine from other fermented vegetables also serve as excellent alternatives. This method ensures a successful fermentation, offering your fruits a delightful tang and fizz.

Notes:

- These fermented berries offer a unique twist to various dishes, serving as an excellent topping for desserts like custard, yogurt, or ice cream, and as a flavorful addition to smoothies. Enjoy the unique taste and health benefits of homemade fermented berries with this simple recipe.

87. HONEY FERMENTED PLUMS

INGREDIENTS:

» 15 to 18 firm red plums, sufficient to fill a 2-quart jar
» Enough filtered water to fill the 2-quart jar once plums are added
» 1 ½ tsp salt
» 6 tbsp raw light honey

» Optional: 1 ½ handfuls currant leaves
» Optional: ¾ tsp cardamom pods
» 3 tbsp active rye sourdough starter or a piece of stale rye bread
» A handful fresh mint leaves
» 1 ½ tbsp whole-grain rye flour

Yield: Approximately 4 pints or a 2-quart jar

INSTRUCTIONS:

1. Begin by layering the plums and, if using, mint and currant leaves inside a 2-quart jar, packing them tightly.
2. To accurately measure the water needed, fill the jar containing the plums. Transfer this water to a medium pot.
3. Add the salt and whole-grain rye flour to the pot of water. Mix well, then bring to a boil. Allow the mixture to cool to room temperature afterward.
4. Once the mixture has cooled, incorporate the raw honey and the active rye sourdough starter into it, stirring thoroughly to create your fermenting brine.
5. Gently pour the prepared brine over the plums in the jar, ensuring the liquid reaches the top.
6. Tightly seal the jars and leave them at room temperature for 5–7 days, opening them daily to skim off any foam that forms on the surface.
7. After 5–7 days, transfer the jars to the refrigerator and allow the ferment to mature for an additional 2–4 weeks before starting to consume the plums.

Notes:

• Currant leaves, especially those from black currants, possess a rich aroma and contribute a distinctive flavor to a variety of lacto-fermented products, including kvass, kombucha, and teas. Cultivating currant bushes for their leaves can be an enriching endeavor for both your kitchen and garden, offering a unique flavor agent for your fermentation projects.

Kimchi

A staple of Korean cuisine with rich flavors and health benefits

Kimchi stands as a cornerstone of Korean gastronomy, celebrated for its robust flavors and numerous health advantages. This fermented medley of vegetables, primarily featuring Napa cabbage alongside radishes, green onions, garlic, ginger, and a distinct variety of chili peppers, distinguishes itself with a unique sour and spicy profile.

The fermentation journey of kimchi, notably swifter than that of sauerkraut, unfolds a rich tapestry of tastes and scents. Crucial to kimchi's texture and flavor is the initial salting of the Napa cabbage, which is crucial for drawing out moisture while maintaining its crunchiness and freshness, thus shortening fermentation time and reducing salt usage.

Kimchi is not only a flavorful accompaniment to meals but also plays a central role in dishes such as stews and pancakes. Its nutritional profile boasts high levels of vitamins A, C, and B complex, alongside a wealth of phytochemicals and probiotics, making it an excellent low-calorie option for enhancing gut health and boosting immunity. Incorporating kimchi into one's diet enriches it with vital nutrients and probiotics amidst a backdrop of authentic, healthy flavors.

The making of kimchi necessitates meticulous cleanliness to foster the growth of beneficial bacteria like Weissella and Lactobacillus species, pivotal for its fermentation. Beginning with brining, this step not only aids in preservation but also allows for a deeper infusion of flavors, achieving a final salt concentration between 2–5%. The vegetables naturally ferment through "wild cultures" present on them, reaching an ideal pH of around 4.2 due to the formation of lactic and acetic acids.

Kimchi's fermentation is relatively rapid, often ready in 1–2 days at room temperature, with an extended period if kept cool. For safety and to preserve its peak quality, kimchi should ideally be refrigerated and enjoyed within a week, as its freshness wanes over extended fermentation periods.

88. TRADITIONAL KOREAN BAECHU KIMCHI

INGREDIENTS:

- » 6–8 lb Napa cabbage (approximately 2 medium-sized cabbages)
- » 2 tbsp sweet rice flour
- » 1 ½ cups coarse sea salt
- » 4 quarts plus ½ cup cold water, divided
- » 1 to 8 garlic cloves, adjusted to taste
- » 1 to 1 ½ lb Korean or daikon radish (about 1 or 2 radishes)
- » 1 Asian pear, optional for added sweetness
- » 3 slices fresh ginger
- » 9 scallions
- » 2 tsp finely ground salt, optional for taste adjustment
- » 1 tsp fish sauce, optional for depth of flavor
- » 1 cup Korean red pepper powder, specifically for kimchi

Yield: Approximately 6 pints

INSTRUCTIONS:

1. Cabbage preparation: Rinse the Napa cabbage and cut it into 2-inch pieces. Soak the pieces briefly in a saltwater solution made from ½ cup salt dissolved in 4 quarts of water, then massage with an additional 1 cup of sea salt. Let the cabbage rest at room temperature for 3–6 hours. Afterward, rinse the cabbage thoroughly and let it drain for about 30 minutes.
2. Seasoning paste: Cook the sweet rice flour with ½ cup water until it thickens, then let it cool. Mix this paste with minced garlic, ginger, and red pepper powder to form the seasoning base.
3. Prepare the vegetables: Julienne the radish, and pear, and slice the scallions.
4. Mixing: Combine the cooled rice flour paste with the julienned vegetables, adding fish sauce and additional salt as needed.

5. Combining: Mix the seasoned paste thoroughly with the drained cabbage to ensure an even coating.
6. Packing: Pack the mixed kimchi into a fermentation container, pressing down firmly to reduce air pockets and leaving some space at the top for expansion. Seal the container and place it on a plate or tray to catch any overflow.
7. Fermentation options: For slow fermentation, refrigerate for 3–4 days. For a quicker fermentation process, let the container sit at room temperature (around 68°F) for 1–2 days.
8. Storage: Keep the kimchi tightly sealed in the refrigerator, pressing down occasionally to keep the vegetables submerged. If mold develops, discard the affected parts.

Notes: The natural bacteria present in the ingredients initiate the fermentation, negating the need for an external starter culture. Kimchi's versatility allows it to complement a wide array of dishes, from simple rice and noodles to more elaborate pancakes and sandwiches. This recipe demystifies the art of making traditional kimchi, inviting you to integrate this nutritious and flavorful Korean staple into your culinary repertoire.

89. EASY KIMCHI RECIPE

INGREDIENTS:
» 1 large Napa cabbage (about 2 ½ lb)
» 5 scallions
» 1 large daikon radish (1 lb)
» 4 garlic cloves
» 2 tbsp sea salt
» 1 tbsp fresh ginger, minced
» ¼ cup red pepper powder (or pepper flakes)
» 2 tbsp fish sauce

Yield: About 4 pints

INSTRUCTIONS:
1. Prepare the vegetables: Chop the cabbage into pieces roughly 2 cm in size, julienne or shred the radish, and finely mince the garlic and ginger.
2. Combine ingredients: In a sizable bowl, thoroughly mix all the ingredients. Spend a few minutes massaging the mixture to integrate the flavors and initiate moisture release.
3. Resting period: Allow the mixture to sit at room temperature for about 30 minutes. This step helps draw out water from the vegetables, crucial for the fermentation process.
4. Jar packing: Tightly pack the kimchi mixture into jars, making sure the vegetables are submerged in their natural juices. Leave approximately 3 cm of space from the top of the jar.
5. Fermentation: Store the jars at room temperature for a minimum of 5 days to ferment. The appearance of bubbles within the jar is a natural sign of fermentation.
6. Storage: Once fermentation is noticed, the kimchi should be refrigerated. Properly stored, it will keep for several months in the fridge.

Notes:
» Ingredient substitutions are welcome but maintain the salt ratio to ensure proper fermentation.
» The flavor profile of kimchi develops and deepens over time; a sour aroma and the formation of fermentation bubbles are indicators of successful fermentation.

This quick kimchi recipe simplifies the traditional process, making it accessible for you to create this flavorful and healthful Korean staple right at home.

90. KIMCHI WITH DAIKON RADISH

INGREDIENTS:

» 3 lb daikon radish, peeled and thinly sliced
» 9 scallions, finely chopped
» 1 piece (1 ½-inch) ginger, thinly sliced into strips
» 6 garlic cloves, thinly sliced
» 6 tbsp gochujang (Korean chili powder)
» 3 tbsp fish sauce
» 3 tbsp fine sea salt

Yield: About 3 pints

INSTRUCTIONS:

1. Mixing: In a medium-sized bowl, mix the daikon radish slices, scallions, ginger strips, and garlic slices. Add the gochujang, fish sauce, and sea salt to the vegetables. Stir everything gently until the mixture is evenly coated. Cover and let it marinate for about 2 hours, allowing the daikon to release its natural juices.
2. Jar filling: Carefully transfer the marinated mixture into a quart-sized mason jar. Press the mixture down firmly to eliminate any air pockets and ensure the vegetables are submerged in their brine.
3. Fermentation: Place a glass weight over the vegetables to keep them submerged below the brine. Seal the jar with a fermentation seal or airlock to allow gases to escape without letting air in. Let the jar ferment at room temperature for 3 days.
4. Refrigeration: Once the fermentation process is complete, transfer the jar to the refrigerator for storage. This will slow down the fermentation process and preserve the kimchi.

Notes: This spicy, tangy, and crunchy daikon radish kimchi is a perfect side dish to complement roasted meats, fried tofu, or grilled fish. Unlike the traditional cubed daikon kimchi, this recipe features thinly sliced daikon for a visually appealing texture and a quicker pickling process. Enjoy the vibrant flavors that this kimchi adds to your meals.

91. KOREAN CUCUMBER KIMCHI

INGREDIENTS:

» 8 small cucumbers (Persian or Kirby varieties)
» 4 tbsp fine sea salt for soaking
» 8 cups hot water
» 1 medium carrot, julienned
» 8 scallions, julienned
» 6 garlic cloves, minced
» 1 tsp fresh ginger, grated
» 4 tbsp gochujang
» 2 tbsp fish sauce
» 1 tbsp unrefined cane sugar
» ¼ cup water
» 1 tsp sea salt

Yield: About 2 pints

INSTRUCTIONS:

1. Prepare cucumbers: Trim the tips and slice each cucumber lengthwise without cutting through the bottom. Place them in a bowl.
2. Soaking: Dissolve 4 tbsp of salt in 8 cups of hot water. Pour over cucumbers, weigh down with a plate, and soak for 2 hours. Then, drain and pat dry.
3. Make filling: In a medium bowl, combine carrot, green onions, garlic, ginger, gochujang, fish sauce, sugar, water, and salt.
4. Fill cucumbers: Stuff each cucumber with the filling and coat the outside. Place stuffed cucumbers in a jar, and cover it with plastic wrap.
5. Fermentation: Leave at room temperature for up to 1 day (or 12 hours if it's hot), then refrigerate for up to 3 days.

Notes: This recipe for cucumber kimchi features crunchy cucumbers filled with a spicy mixture. The kimchi gains a mild, slightly sour taste after a short fermentation. It serves as an ideal, refreshing side dish, especially in warmer months.

Variations:

- **No-Ferment option:** You can opt to enjoy this kimchi fresh, without fermenting, as an immediate side dish.

- **Vegan adaptation:** To make it vegan, substitute the fish sauce with soy sauce or Korean fermented soybean paste.

Miso & Tempeh

Dive into the rich world of fermented foods with a focus on Miso and Tempeh, two Asian culinary marvels known for their unique flavors and health benefits. These fermented foods are staples in their native cultures, offering not only depth to various dishes but also numerous well-being advantages.

Miso

Miso is a cornerstone of Japanese cuisine, celebrated for its complex umami flavor. This fermented soybean paste, enriched with the koji fungus, plays a vital role in the culinary landscape, particularly in soups and sauces.

- *Ingredients & fermentation process:* Crafting miso at home requires koji (rice inoculated with *Aspergillus oryzae*), soybeans, sea salt, and a small amount of existing miso as a starter. The magic of miso lies in its fermentation, a delicate process facilitated by enzymes and beneficial microorganisms. While initial preparation is straightforward, the fermentation journey demands patience, typically ranging from a few weeks to several months.
- *Varieties & flavor exploration:* Miso comes in several varieties, each offering a different flavor profile. Red miso undergoes a lengthy fermentation process, often up to 11 months, delivering a robust taste. In contrast, white miso, with a shorter fermentation period of a few weeks, offers a sweeter and milder flavor. Adventurous cooks might experiment by incorporating other ingredients like chickpeas, buckwheat, mushrooms, or seaweed to create unique miso varieties.
- *Health Benefits:* Beyond its culinary uses, miso is a powerhouse of nutrition. Its fermentation process enhances protein digestibility and bioavailability. Miso is a rich source of essential minerals such as zinc, manganese, and potassium, along with vitamins B2 and B12. It's also packed with probiotics, promoting gut health and supporting the immune system. Research highlights miso's potential in managing blood pressure, providing radiation resistance, and offering cancer-preventive properties.

To create your miso paste, begin with rice koji and soybeans. The fermentation will yield a flavorful paste in six months, with an option to extend the fermentation for a year or more to deepen the taste profile.

92. MISO MADE AT HOME

Begin the fulfilling adventure of homemade miso with this comprehensive tutorial. Miso, a fundamental element in Japanese culinary traditions, serves both as a taste enhancer and a source of nutrition. This guide details the classic method of fermenting soybeans with koji rice, guiding you step by step.

EQUIPMENT NEEDED:

» A large bowl or jar for soaking soybeans.
» Pressure cooker (optional, for quicker cooking).
» Meat grinder or potato masher for processing beans.
» Parchment paper or cling film for covering.
» A large 1-gallon glass container for fermentation.
» Fermentation weights (1–1 ½ kg per kg of miso) to ensure an anaerobic environment. Options include freezer bags filled with salt, ceramic or glass weights, or a small plate with water bottles.

INGREDIENTS:

» 4 cups soybeans
» 4 cups koji rice
» 1 cup sea salt
» 2 tbsp unpasteurized miso (optional, to kick-start fermentation)
» Additional salt for weight (about 10 cups if using a salt-filled freezer bag as a weight)

INSTRUCTIONS:

1. Soybean preparation: Thoroughly rinse and soak soybeans for 12–18 hours. Rinse again and drain. Boil until tender (4–6 hours) or use a pressure cooker to reduce the time. Reserve 1 quart of cooking water and cool the beans.
2. Making the Miso paste: Grind or mash the cooled beans to a paste, ensuring it's not too fine. In a large bowl, mix the bean paste with koji rice, sea salt, and optional unpasteurized miso. Add reserved cooking water to achieve a dough-like consistency.
3. Jarring process: Sterilize the fermentation jar with boiling water, and coat the interior with salt. Form the mixture into balls, throwing them into the jar to remove air pockets. Compress firmly to eliminate spaces. Flatten the top, sprinkle with salt, and cover with parchment paper or cling film, adding salt at the edges. Place the chosen weight on top, ensuring complete coverage, and seal the jar.

4. Fermentation: Label the jar with the date and contents. Store in a stable, cool spot away from direct sunlight for a minimum of 6 months. Longer fermentation yields deeper flavors.
5. Regular checks: Inspect the miso periodically for signs of mold. A slight darkening is normal due to oxidation.
6. Handling mold: White mold is usually harmless and can be scraped off. Other colors may indicate spoilage and the miso should be discarded.
7. Preventing spoilage: Proper sanitation and accurate salt measurements are key to successful fermentation.

Notes:

» Both fresh and dehydrated koji are suitable for this recipe. Adjust the water content to get the right texture.

» It's possible to enjoy part of the miso early on while continuing to ferment the remainder for a richer flavor profile.

» This homemade miso recipe offers a delightful way to introduce traditional fermented foods into your diet, enhancing both the taste and healthfulness of your meals.

Tempeh

Tempeh, originating from Indonesia, stands out in the world of vegetarian cuisine for its substantial texture and impressive nutritional profile. This fermented soybean cake is celebrated as a versatile and protein-rich meat alternative, seamlessly integrating into a myriad of dishes.

The Art of Crafting Tempeh

Creating tempeh involves soaking soybeans, cooking them, and then inoculating them with *Rhizopus oligosporus*, a specific tempeh starter. This fermentation, lasting 24 to 48 hours, transforms the beans into a cohesive, nutrient-dense cake.

Nutritional Boon

Tempeh excels as a source of complete protein, dietary fiber, essential vitamins, and minerals, enhancing diet quality for vegetarians and vegans alike. The fermentation process not only boosts its digestibility but also reduces phytic acid, aiding mineral absorption. Rich in prebiotics, tempeh supports gut health, while its low saturated fat and absence of cholesterol contribute to cardiovascular well-being.

Culinary Versatility

Tempeh's culinary adaptability is remarkable. Whether grilled, fried, steamed, or incorporated into soups and stews, it absorbs flavors like soy, garlic, chili, and ginger beautifully. From curries and stir-fries to salads and sandwiches, tempeh's neutral taste and hearty texture make it an excellent substitute for meat across various cuisines.

Digestive Comfort

For those who find beans challenging to digest, tempeh presents a gentle alternative. Its fermentation process breaks down complex nutrients, rendering it more digestible and less likely to cause discomfort.

Incorporating tempeh into your meals not only diversifies your culinary repertoire but also enriches your diet with essential nutrients and probiotics. Whether you're exploring vegetarian cooking or simply seeking healthful, flavorful food options, tempeh offers a wholesome and satisfying choice.

93. MAKING TEMPEH AT HOME

Craft your tempeh with this simple recipe, harnessing the power of fermentation to create a nutritious, plant-based protein source. Tempeh, originating from Indonesia, is a fermented soy product known for its firm texture and rich, nutty flavor.

INGREDIENTS:

- » 3 cups organic soybeans
- » 4 quarts water (divided for soaking and cooking)
- » 3 tbsp brown rice vinegar
- » 1 tsp tempeh starter
- » large Ziploc bag

INSTRUCTIONS:

1. Soak and clean soybeans: Soak the soybeans in 2 quarts of water for 12–18 hours. Rub the beans between your hands to split them and remove the skins. Rinse several times until most of the skins are removed.
2. Cook soybeans: In a pressure cooker, cook the soybeans with the remaining 2 quarts of water for 12 minutes, or simmer them for 45–60 minutes until they are tender but still firm. Drain and spread them on a towel-lined tray to cool. Allow the soybeans to dry and cool completely.
3. Prepare soybeans for fermentation: Once cooled, mix the soybeans in a bowl with the brown rice vinegar and tempeh starter, ensuring an even distribution.
4. Bagging process: Transfer the soybean mixture into a gallon-size Ziploc bag. Press out as much air as possible before sealing. Flatten the beans into an even layer. Using a cutting board, gently press down to ensure uniform thickness. Puncture the bag all over with a toothpick, flipping and repeating on the other side for adequate air circulation.
5. Fermentation: Place the prepared bag on a wire rack in a warm, dark location, such as an oven preheated to 95–100°F and then turned off, for 12–48 hours. Maintain a consistent temperature of 84–89°F to support rhizopus growth, avoiding frequent opening of the fermentation space.
6. Monitoring growth: Expect to see white mycelium growth within 12–24 hours. The tempeh is ready when it solidifies into a cake and is fully covered in white mold, typically within 36–48 hours, depending on the ambient temperature.

7. Remove and store: Carefully open the bag, remove the tempeh block, and slice according to your preference. Refrigerate for up to 4 days or freeze for up to 3 months.

Notes:

» A nutty, mushroom-like aroma indicates properly fermented tempeh. Discard any tempeh with an off smell, as it suggests contamination.

» Grey or black spots are normal and safe, but the presence of green or pink mold indicates spoilage. In such cases, the tempeh should be discarded immediately for safety reasons.

This homemade tempeh recipe offers a fulfilling way to explore the art of fermentation, providing a wholesome, high-protein addition to your culinary repertoire

94. SPICY MUSTARD FERMENTED

Craft your own bold and tangy mustard with this simple fermentation process. Perfect for enhancing your dishes, this homemade mustard not only brings heat and depth to your meals but also adds a probiotic punch.

INGREDIENTS:

- » ½ cup white wine vinegar
- » 2 tsp honey
- » 4 tbsp yellow mustard seed powder
- » ½ cup whole brown mustard seeds

- » ½ cup whole yellow mustard seeds
- » 1 cup cold water
- » 2 tbsp fine sea salt
- » ½ cup starter culture (options detailed below)

Yield: Approximately 2 pints (in a 2-quart jar)

INSTRUCTIONS:

1. Seed preparation: Coarsely grind the brown and yellow mustard seeds with a spice grinder until just cracked. Transfer the cracked seeds to a pint-sized jar.
2. Mixing: Add cold water and your chosen starter culture to the jar with the seeds. Stir thoroughly to combine.
3. Fermentation: Seal the jar and let it sit at room temperature for three days to ferment.
4. Final touches: Once fermented, open the jar and incorporate the white wine vinegar and honey. Stir well.
5. Storage: Keep the mustard refrigerated. It will stay fresh and flavorful for up to six months.

Fermentation Tips:

- Quality spices: The key to exceptional mustard lies in using high-quality spices.
- Grind size: Ensure the mustard seeds are coarsely ground; you're aiming to crack them open rather than pulverize them.
- Consistency: Initially, the mustard might seem too liquid, but it will thicken throughout fermentation.
- Starter culture: Utilize a starter culture like vegetable brine, kombucha, or fresh whey from yogurt/kefir. These introduce beneficial bacteria to jumpstart fermentation.
- Customization: Feel free to add personal touches such as shallots, garlic, or herbs to suit your taste. Experimentation is encouraged once you're comfortable with the basics.

Choosing a Starter Culture:

- Vegetable brine: The leftover brine from fermented vegetables is an excellent choice.
- Fresh whey: Extracted from yogurt or kefir, whey is teeming with beneficial bacteria.
- Kombucha: Its vinegary taste and bacterial content make kombucha an ideal starter.
- Packaged starter cultures: Available in powder form, these cultures are designed specifically for fermentation.

Creating your fermented mustard is a straightforward and rewarding endeavor. With just a few ingredients and a bit of patience, you can produce a condiment that's not only delicious but also healthful, thanks to its probiotic content.

95. CRANBERRY RELISH FERMENTED

Elevate your condiment game with this vibrant and tangy cranberry-orange relish. Fermented to perfection, this relish combines the freshness of cranberries and oranges with the depth of shallots and rosemary, finished with rich balsamic vinegar.

INGREDIENTS:

» 3 cups fresh cranberries
» 1 cup raisins
» 2 organic oranges (essential for using the skin)

» 4 tbsp diced shallots (about 2 small ones)
» 2 tsp salt
» 2 tbsp chopped rosemary
» For finishing: 2 tbsp balsamic vinegar

Yield: Approximately 2 pints

INSTRUCTIONS:

1. Prepare the fruit: Wash the oranges thoroughly. Cut into 8 wedges, removing seeds. Check the cranberries, removing any that are wrinkled or damaged.
2. Blend the mixture: In a blender or food processor, combine orange pieces (including the peel), cranberries, raisins, shallots, rosemary, and salt. Pulse until coarsely chopped, retaining some texture since it's a relish.
3. Ferment: Transfer the mixture to a glass jar. Cover with a tea towel, coffee filter, or loosely fitting lid, and store in a dark place, like a cupboard, for 24 hours. Stir daily if fermenting longer, but 24 hours is typically sufficient for the flavors to blend without becoming overly sour.
4. Finish with vinegar: After fermentation, stir in the balsamic vinegar. Adjust sweetness if desired, with additional sugar or maple syrup (see notes).
5. Storage: Keep the relish in an airtight container in the refrigerator, ideally consumed within a month for the best freshness.

Notes:

» This cranberry relish naturally balances tartness with sweetness, courtesy of the raisins. For those desiring a sweeter profile, consider adding up to ¼ cup of sugar for balance, or up to ½ cup for a sweeter relish. Adjust to taste.

» This relish pairs wonderfully with turkey, brie cheese, or as a unique sandwich spread. Its blend of savory and sweet flavors, enhanced by the fermentation process, makes it a healthy and flavorful addition to any meal.

Enjoy the delightful combination of cranberries and oranges in this homemade fermented relish, a perfect blend of tangy, sweet, and savory elements that will make a memorable addition to your culinary creations.

96. TOMATO AND JALAPEÑO FERMENTED SALSA

Unleash the flavors of fresh vegetables with this spicy fermented salsa, a perfect blend of Roma tomatoes, jalapeños, and aromatic herbs. This recipe not only offers a zesty kick to your dishes but also introduces beneficial probiotics to your diet.

INGREDIENTS:

» 1 ½ medium white onions, diced
» 12 medium Roma tomatoes, cored, seeded, and diced
» 4–5 garlic cloves, finely chopped
» 4–5 medium Jalapeños, finely chopped
» 1 cup cilantro, finely chopped
» 1 ½ limes juiced
» 1 ½ tbsp fine sea salt
» ½ cup starter culture or water

Yield: Approximately 3 pints

INSTRUCTIONS:

1. Combine ingredients: Start with fresh, quality produce. In a large bowl, combine the tomatoes, onions, garlic, jalapeños, cilantro, and lime juice. Season with the sea salt and allow to sit for about 15 minutes, letting the vegetables marinate and release their juices. Use gloves when handling the Jalapeños to avoid skin irritation.
2. Incorporate starter culture: If utilizing a starter culture, mix it into your salsa now. This step introduces beneficial bacteria to aid in fermentation.
3. Jar preparation: Carefully spoon the salsa mixture into a glass jar, pressing down gently to remove air pockets and ensure the salsa is well-packed.
4. Cover with liquid: Make sure the salsa is completely submerged in its juice to prevent mold. Add any remaining liquid from the bowl, additional starter culture, or a saltwater solution if necessary.
5. Weight down: Place fermentation weights over the salsa to keep the contents submerged below the liquid. If you don't have weights, you can use a smaller jar filled with water as a makeshift weight. Ensure the jar is sealed properly, and if using a non-airtight method, remember to 'burp' the jar twice daily.
6. Ferment: Store the jar in a spot out of direct sunlight, where the temperature is consistent. Ferment for about 3 days, though timing may vary based on the ambient temperature of your kitchen.
7. Refrigerate: Once fermentation is complete, move the salsa to the refrigerator. It will keep well for several weeks.

Enjoy this spicy fermented salsa as a vibrant addition to your meals, bringing a probiotic boost along with its fiery flavor. Ideal for tacos, grilled meats, or as a dip, this salsa is sure to become a staple in your culinary repertoire.

97. HOT SAUCE LACTO-FERMENTED

Elevate your hot sauce game with this homemade lacto-fermented version, boasting a complex flavor profile and a tangy twist. Perfect for chili enthusiasts looking to explore beyond commercial Sriracha, this sauce marries heat with depth, courtesy of a mix of aromatic vegetables.

INGREDIENTS:

» 1 pound your preferred hot chilies
» ½ onion
» 4 carrots

» 4 garlic cloves
» 4 tsp fine sea salt
» Water, enough to cover the vegetables in the jar

Yield: Approximately 2 pints

INSTRUCTIONS:

1. Vegetable preparation: With gloves on, trim the stems from the chilies. For a milder sauce, remove seeds and membranes. Peel and slice the carrots. Chop the onion into large chunks, and peel the garlic cloves.
2. Jar layering: In a clean jar, layer the chilies, carrots, onion, and garlic. Sprinkle evenly with sea salt. Fill the jar with water, ensuring all vegetables are submerged.
3. Fermentation setup: Place a glass weight over the vegetables to keep them below the brine. Seal the jar with an airlock lid. Allow the jar to ferment at room temperature for 2–3 weeks, checking periodically.
4. Blend the sauce: Once fermented, remove the vegetables from the brine (save the brine). Blend the vegetables until smooth, adding reserved brine as needed to achieve your preferred consistency.
5. Storage: Pour the finished sauce into a clean glass jar. Store in a cool, dark place or refrigerate.

Notes:

» This lacto-fermented hot sauce can be stored for several months in the fridge.
» The leftover brine is flavorful and can be used to enhance dressings, soups, or other ferments.

» Customize your hot sauce by adding different aromatics or fruits to the fermentation jar. Experiment with ingredients like ginger, mango, or pineapple for unique flavor combinations.

Enjoy this homemade hot sauce with your favorite meals, knowing you've created a probiotic-rich condiment that's as healthy as it is delicious. Whether drizzled over tacos, mixed into marinades, or served alongside cheese platters, this lacto-fermented chili sauce is sure to impress.

98. WORCESTERSHIRE SAUCE MADE AT HOME

Why we love Worcestershire sauce: The magical touch in cooking!

Worcestershire sauce is that magical touch that can transform any savory dish. It's perfect for reviving bland soups or lackluster chili. Used in a wide range of recipes, from braised meats to vegetables, soups, savory pies, salad dressings, marinades, and even Bloody Mary, this sauce is a true kitchen all-rounder. It adds a unique mix of umami (that irresistible rich flavor), acidity, and a hint of sweetness, working well as an alternative to soy sauce or fish sauce. With Worcestershire sauce, it's easy to give a special touch to any dish!

INGREDIENTS:

» 1 ½ onions, roughly sliced
» 3 fluid ounces boiling water
» 6 tbsp tamarind paste
» 3-ounce can anchovies
» 12 tbsp unsulfured molasses
» 1 ½-inch piece fresh ginger, peeled & chopped
» 6 tbsp raisins
» 3 cardamom pods

» 3 cups white vinegar or apple vinegar
» 3 tbsp kosher or canning salt
» 3 tbsp Maple syrup or brown sugar
» 1 ½ tbsp dry mustard
» 1 ½ tsp whole cloves
» ¾ tsp ground cinnamon
» 1 ½ tsp black peppercorns
» 9–12 garlic cloves, crushed
» 1 ½ tbsp crushed red pepper flakes

Yield: about 2–3 pints/ 1 ½-quart jar

INSTRUCTIONS:

1. Raisin preparation: Start by soaking the raisins in boiling water for 15 minutes to soften. Drain and discard the water afterward.
2. Blending ingredients: In a food processor, blend the softened raisins, molasses, tamarind paste, anchovies, onions, ginger, garlic, and half the vinegar until smooth.
3. Cooking mixture: Pour the puree into a saucepan, and add the remaining ingredients, including the rest of the vinegar. Bring to a boil, then remove from heat.
4. Canning: Carefully transfer the hot mixture into a 1 ½-quart canning jar. Secure with a plastic lid and store in a cool, dark place for at least one month to allow the flavors to meld. For a deeper flavor, consider extending the maturation period.
5. Final touches: When you're ready to enjoy, strain the sauce through a fine-mesh sieve to remove any solids.

Notes:

» The choice of vinegar can subtly influence the final taste of your Worcestershire sauce. Opt for apple vinegar for a sweet, fruity undertone, or white wine vinegar for a traditional, tangy profile.

99. KETCHUP FERMENTED AT HOME

Elevate your condiment repertoire with this artisanal fermented ketchup. This homemade version not only surpasses store-bought varieties in taste but also enriches your meals with probiotics, thanks to the fermentation process.

INGREDIENTS:

- » 4 cans tomato paste (or 3 cups homemade tomato paste)
- » 6 tbsp raw vinegar (either store-bought or homemade)
- » 6 tbsp maple syrup or raw honey
- » 1 ½ tbsp soy sauce (or Worcestershire sauce), adjusted to taste
- » 1 tsp sea salt
- » 4 tbsp whey or brine from existing vegetable ferments
- » ¼ tsp allspice
- » ¼ tsp black pepper

Yield: Approximately 2 pints (1-quart jar)

INSTRUCTIONS:

1. Probiotic note: To ensure your ketchup is rich in probiotics, utilize real whey (not powdered) or brine from an existing ferment, such as sauerkraut.
2. Mixing: In a bowl, thoroughly combine all the ingredients. Adjust the seasonings according to your preference.
3. Jar preparation and fermentation: Transfer the mixture into a quart-sized mason jar. You can use either an airlock for a fuss-free fermentation or a regular lid—just remember to "burp" the jar daily to release built-up gases.
4. Room temperature fermentation: Allow the ketchup to ferment at room temperature for 2–3 days. This step initiates the fermentation process, enhancing the flavor and probiotic content.
5. Refrigeration: After the initial fermentation period, place the ketchup in the refrigerator for an additional three days to slow down the fermentation and stabilize the flavor.
6. Serving suggestions: This ketchup is perfect with a variety of dishes, from homemade burgers and hash browns to classic French fries.
7. Storage: Properly stored in the refrigerator, the ketchup can last between 3–6 months. While freezing is possible, refrigeration is recommended to preserve the probiotic benefits. Note that canning, although it extends shelf life, will eliminate the beneficial bacteria.

Notes:

- » If the ketchup thickens more than desired after fermentation, you can adjust the consistency by adding 1–2 tbsp of water, either during the mixing stage or after fermentation.

Dairy and Bread

Bakery delights and dairy products—sourdough, gluten-free bread, kefir, homemade butter, cream and cheese:

Welcome to the delightful world of bread-making and dairy fermentation, a place where the warmth of tradition meets the spark of innovation in every recipe. Dive into the age-old craft of sourdough and naturally leavened breads, and discover contemporary alternatives like gluten-free bread, perfect for various dietary needs. I'm here to guide you through the process of baking aromatic, full-bodied breads, from timeless classics to gluten-free options. You'll learn how to start and maintain a sourdough starter, a crucial element for any home-baked bread.

Moreover, uncover the art of crafting smooth kefir, homemade butter, cream, and cheese—hallmarks of thoughtful, wholesome cooking. This journey is for anyone eager to blend flavor, health, and the satisfaction of making something beautiful with their own hands.

100. RECIPE FOR STARTING SOURDOUGH

INGREDIENTS:

» ¾ cup (4 ounces) all-purpose flour (daily)
» ½ cup (4 ounces) bottled unchlorinated water

1

2

3

4-5

Consistent growth

INSTRUCTIONS:

1. Day 1: Initial mix: Start assembling the ingredients to create the initial starter. Measure the flour and water accurately using a kitchen scale. Combine the flour and water in a 2-quart glass container, ensuring room for growth. Stir until smooth. Cover the container lightly and place it in a warm spot (70 to 75°F). Let it rest for 24 hours.
2. Day 2: First feeding: You might not notice much change. Discard half of the starter. Add fresh flour and water, mix well, and let it sit for another day.
3. Day 3: Signs of life: Look for bubbles and a thicker consistency, indicating activity. Repeat the feeding process from Day 2.
4. Day 4: Increased activity: The mixture should be very bubbly with a stronger sour scent. Continue the discard and feed cycle.
5. Day 5: Starter is ready: The starter should now be active, with plenty of bubbles and a pronounced aroma. It's ready for baking or maintenance.

Yeast Readiness Indicators:

» **Size and bubbles:** The starter should double in size with visible bubbles.
» **Timing:** Typically, doubling occurs about 12 hours after feeding at 68°F, but this can vary.
» **Aroma and texture:** Expect a tangy smell and fluffy texture.
» **Float test:** Drop a spoonful of starter in water; if it floats, it's ready.
» **Consistent growth:** A starter that reliably grows after feeding is a good sign.

Sourdough Starter Maintenance & Tips

» Ensuring the longevity and vitality of your sourdough starter is crucial for consistently baking delicious sourdough bread.

Here's a guide to maintaining your starter healthy, active, and ready for all your baking adventures.

Routine Maintenance:

» **Daily care:** If kept at room temperature, maintain a balanced 1:1 ratio of flour to water by volume. Regularly discard half of the starter and replenish it with 4 ounces of flour and 4 ounces of water. It keeps the starter fresh and active for immediate use.

» **Use in baking:** When your starter is bubbly and vigorous, it's perfect for baking. Use the portion you would otherwise discard for your favorite sourdough recipes.

» **Refrigeration for infrequent use:** For those who bake less often, the starter can be thickened with a double portion of flour (8 ounces) to 4 ounces of water and stored in the fridge with a loose lid. This thicker mix slows down the fermentation, requiring only weekly feeding.

Additional Tips for Success:

» **Temperature sensitivity:** Starters are highly responsive to temperature. In warmer conditions, your starter may mature faster than anticipated, potentially ready in under five days. In cooler environments, seek a warmer spot or insulate your container to maintain an optimal fermentation temperature.

» **Monitoring activity:** An active starter will show signs of life through bubbling and expansion. If these signs are lacking, increase the frequency of feedings to encourage activity.

» **Reviving refrigerated starters:** If your starter has been in the fridge and appears sluggish, let it warm to room temperature and resume the regular feeding schedule until it shows consistent growth.

» **Health checks:** Keep an eye out for any off smells or unusual colors. These could indicate contamination, at which point it's safer to discard the starter and start fresh.

Creating a sourdough starter is a simple yet fascinating process, connecting you to the timeless art of bread-making. This living ingredient not only leavens bread but also imbues it with flavor, texture, and nutritional benefits. Enjoy the journey to your first home-baked sourdough loaf!

101. CLASSIC SOURDOUGH BREAD

Embrace the art of natural leavening with this comprehensive recipe. Perfecting sourdough bread involves cultivating your starter and understanding the subtle interplay between flour, water, and time. Let's embark on this journey into baking together.

INGREDIENTS

for making ¼ cup (50g) active sourdough starter

- » 2 tsp sourdough starter
- » 3 tbsp all-purpose flour
- » 5 tsp water

INGREDIENTS OF THE DOUGH:

- » ¼–½ cup (50–100g) active sourdough starter (depending on your environment, see note)
- » 1 ½ cups warm water
- » 4 cups bread flour
- » 1 ½–2 tsp fine sea salt

INSTRUCTIONS:

1. Feed your Sourdough starter: Around 12 hours before you plan to make your dough, prepare ¼ cup (50g) of active sourdough starter. To do this, put the starter ingredients into a clean jar and mix them well. Cover the jar loosely and leave it at room temperature to ferment. This action will yield approximately 60g of starter, taking into account that some will stick to the sides of the jar. You'll know the starter is ready to use when it has significantly increased in volume and is bubbly at the top and along the sides of the jar.

2. Mixing the dough: In a large bowl, blend the active starter with 1 ½ cups of warm water. Add 4 cups flour and 1 ½ to 2 tsp sea salt into a shaggy dough. Cover and rest for 30 minutes.

3. Stretch and fold: After resting, perform a series of stretches and folds, pulling the dough from the corners towards the center. Repeat this process 3–4 times, resting 30 minutes between each session.

4. Bulk fermentation (1° rise): Allow the dough to rise by covering the bowl with plastic wrap or a damp kitchen towel, then placing it in a warm spot. The dough is ready for the next step when it has doubled in size and looks less dense. This process can take anywhere from 8 to 12 hours, depending on several factors such as the temperature of the ingredients, the activity level of the starter, and the temperature and humidity of your kitchen. For example, during warmer months, the dough might only need 2–4 hours to rise at 85° F (29°C), but in cooler conditions, it could require 10–12 hours at 68° F (20°C).

5. Shaping: Gently shape the dough into a round loaf on a lightly floured surface, creating tension by folding the top towards the center.

6. Rest: Let the shaped dough rest seam-side up in a floured bowl for 30 minutes. Prepare a lined basket for the final proof.

7. Proofing (2° rise): After resting, place the dough seam side up in the prepared basket. Cover and refrigerate for 1 to 48 hours. Longer proofing enhances flavor and texture. The longer the dough is left to proof in the refrigerator, the lighter and more aerated the crumb of the bread will be (see note).

8. Preheat and bake: Preheat your oven with a Dutch oven inside to 550°F (290°C). Slash the dough, place it on parchment in the Dutch oven, reduce to 450°F (230°C), and bake covered for 30 minutes. Uncover, reduce to 400°F (200°C), and bake for an additional 10–15 minutes.

9. Cooling: Allow the bread to cool on a wire rack for at least 1 hour before slicing.

Note and Tips:

» Adjust the amount of starter based on your kitchen's temperature and desired fermentation time.

» A straight-sided vessel helps monitor dough expansion.

» Experiment with salt quantity for flavor adjustment.

» A long, cold-proof (minimum 25 hours) yields a superior texture and flavor, with a more open crumb.

» Preheating the Dutch oven ensures a crisp crust.

Sourdough bread-making is a rewarding process that invites experimentation and patience. Each loaf is a testament to the time and care invested, yielding a deeply flavorful bread, with a satisfying texture and crust. Enjoy the process and the delicious outcomes of your sourdough-baking adventures!

102. STARTER FOR GLUTEN-FREE SOURDOUGH

Creating a gluten-free sourdough starter is a simple process that opens up a world of baking possibilities for those avoiding gluten. This starter uses brown rice flour, which is readily available and yields a robust and versatile sourdough culture.

INGREDIENTS:

» 6 cups brown rice flour (for feeding over several days)

» Water

INSTRUCTIONS:

1. Day 1: Starting your culture. Mix ½ cup of brown rice flour with ¼ cup of water in a clean jar. Stir until well combined, cover loosely (allowing air in but keeping contaminants out), and let it rest at room temperature for 24 hours.
2. Day 2: Stir. Stir the mixture from Day 1, re-cover loosely, and leave at room temperature for another 24 hours. This aerates the mixture, encouraging fermentation.
3. Day 3: Feed. Add another ½ cup of brown rice flour and ¼ cup of water to the jar. Mix thoroughly, cover loosely, and allow it to ferment for another day.
4. Day 4 to 7: Daily feeding and observation. Each day, remove half of the mixture from the jar to avoid accumulation and ensure vigorous fermentation. Add to the jar ½ cup of brown rice flour and ¼ cup of water daily, mixing well. Cover loosely and leave at room temperature. Use a rubber band to mark the starter level after feeding to monitor its growth. The starter is deemed active and ready for baking when it shows a 20–25% increase in volume within 6–12 hours after feeding, accompanied by bubbles indicating fermentation.

Maintenance Notes:

» Storage: When not in use, store the starter in the refrigerator to slow down fermentation. Activate it the night before baking by taking it out, feeding it, and allowing it to ferment at room temperature.

» Weekly care: Maintain your starter's health by discarding half of it once a week and feeding it with ½ cup of gluten-free flour and ¼ cup of water. Then, return it to the fridge.

» Using discard: Keep the discarded portion of the starter in a separate container in the fridge. This "discard" can be used in various gluten-free recipes, offering a tangy flavor and reducing waste.

103. GLUTEN-FREE SOURDOUGH BREAD

Discover the joy of baking with this gluten-free sourdough bread recipe, where natural yeast meets a blend of gluten-free flour to create a loaf that's as soft and tasty as its wheat-based counterpart. Perfect for those with gluten sensitivities or anyone looking to explore the world of gluten-free baking.

INGREDIENTS FOR ACTIVATING THE STARTER:

- » ½ cup (125g) unfed gluten-free sourdough starter
- » ¼ cup (60g) water
- » ½ cup (70g) brown rice flour

DRY INGREDIENTS:

- » 1 ½ cups (210g) brown rice flour
- » ½ cup (60g) cornstarch
- » 1 cup (120g) tapioca flour
- » 2 ½ tsp (8g) xanthan gum
- » 2 tbsp (16g) psyllium husks
- » 1 tbsp baking powder
- » 2 tsp (10g) salt

WET INGREDIENTS:

- » 1 cup (250g) active gluten-free sourdough starter
- » 2 tbsp (10g) ground flaxseed
- » 1 ½ cups + 2 tbsp (390g) water
- » ¼ cup (60g) olive oil
- » 1 tsp (5g) apple cider vinegar
- » 1 tbsp (20g) honey (or agave, maple syrup)

INSTRUCTIONS:

Feeding your starter:

1. Prepare the starter: Combine the starter ingredients in a jar 12 hours before making your dough. Stir well, cover loosely, and let it rise at room temperature until it's bubbly and has increased by 30%.

Making the dough:

2. Wet ingredients: In a bowl, whisk together water, ground flaxseed, active sourdough starter, honey, olive oil, and apple cider vinegar.
3. Dry ingredients: In a stand mixer with a paddle attachment, mix brown rice flour, tapioca flour, cornstarch, psyllium husks, xanthan gum, salt, and baking powder for 1–2 minutes.
4. Combine: Gradually incorporate the wet ingredients into the dry mix. Beat on low for 5 minutes, until the dough is thick but pliable. Adjust consistency with additional water if necessary.
5. Rise: Transfer the dough to a parchment-lined 9" x 5" loaf pan. Let it rise in a warm place until it slightly domes above the pan, approximately 5–13 hours, depending on your kitchen's temperature.

Baking:

6. Preheat the oven: Preheat your oven to 375°F (190°C). Score the top of the dough with a sharp knife.
7. Bake: Place the dough in the oven and bake for 60 minutes, or until golden and hollow-sounding when tapped.
8. Cool: Immediately remove from the pan and cool on a wire rack before slicing.

Notes:

- » Storage: Bread can be stored at room temperature in a sealed container for up to 3 days or frozen for up to 3 months.
- » Flour substitution: For an alternative flour blend, use 3 cups (372g) of a commercial gluten-free flour mix, adjust the xanthan gum to 2 tsp, and water to 1 ¾ cups (420g) total.

This gluten-free sourdough bread offers a delightful alternative to traditional wheat bread, maintaining the beloved textures and flavors without the gluten. Whether you're celiac, gluten-sensitive, or simply curious, this recipe promises a satisfying baking and eating experience.

Kefir: Uses and Maintenance

Kefir stands out as a powerhouse of health benefits, known for its ability to enhance digestion, boost immunity, and even offer anti-cancer properties. Rich in vitamins and minerals, kefir adds nutritional value to a variety of fermented foods and drinks.

Types of Kefirs

- *Vegan kefir (water kefir):* Utilizes SCOBY (Symbiotic Culture of Bacteria and Yeast) grains to ferment sugars in water, creating a non-dairy, carbonated beverage.
- *Dairy kefir:* Produced using specific grains that ferment dairy products, resulting in a tangy, yogurt-like drink.

Kefir Grains and Their Use

- *Live grains:* These can be used repeatedly and are available in both wet and dehydrated forms.
- *Powdered culture starter:* Offers a finite number of uses (up to 7), providing a convenient option for fermenting liquids without the need for live grains.

Using Kefir

Kefir's versatility extends to fermenting drinks, such as sodas and yogurt-like beverages, as well as pickles and condiments. It can also serve as a whey substitute in recipes, offering a smoother fermentation process.

Preparing and Storing Kefir Grains

- *Wet grains:* Should be used immediately.
- *Dry grains:* Require rehydration in warm water before use.
- *Storage:* Inactive grains can be stored in water in the fridge or dehydrated for longer preservation.

Using Body Ecology Kefir Starter

1. *First use:* Dissolve a packet in a quart of lukewarm coconut or sugar-sweetened water. Ensure the water is around skin temperature (92°F).
2. *Fermentation:* Stir well, cover, and allow fermenting at room temperature for 24–48 hours before refrigerating.

Key Maintenance and Usage Points

- *Growth indicators:* Healthy kefir grains will grow and multiply. If you're satisfied with your fermented products, you're on the right track. Discard any batches with mold.
- *Fermentation timeline:* Grains typically ferment liquids within 2 days to a week. Regularly start new batches with the grains.
- *Storage options:* To manage frequent use, live grains can be stored in the fridge to slow fermentation or dehydrated for long-term storage.
- *Starter alternatives:* Body Ecology's Starter is a convenient option for those preferring not to maintain live cultures, requiring a break after 8 generations, unlike live grains which can be used indefinitely.
- *Experimentation:* Lacking grains or starters, you can experiment with water and probiotic powders or veggie culture starters for some fermentations.
- *Sharing surplus grains:* If you find yourself with an excess of live grains, consider sharing them with interested friends or fermentation communities.

Embracing kefir in your diet not only contributes to a healthier gut microbiome but also allows for creative culinary experiments, from beverages to baked goods. Whether you opt for vegan or dairy kefir, the process of fermenting and maintaining your cultures can be a rewarding journey into the world of probiotic foods.

Kefir Grains Storage and Usage Guide

Unlock the potential of kefir grains with this comprehensive guide, ensuring you maximize their health benefits, flavor, and longevity.

Storing kefir grains:

- *Immediate Use:* Ideal to use grains immediately for a new fermentation to maintain vitality.

Fridge storage:

- Grains can be stored in the fridge for up to 3 weeks.
- Drain the grains, place them in an airtight container, cover them with water, add 1 tsp of sugar, and refrigerate. Drain before next use.

Freezer storage:

- For longer storage, grains can be frozen for up to 6 months.
- Dry the grains thoroughly, place them in an airtight bag, and freeze. Note that frequent freezing or refrigeration may weaken the grains over time.

Flavoring water kefir:

- Enhance water kefir by adding fruit juice, herbal teas, chopped fruit, or spices after the grains are removed to prevent contamination.

Fermentation success indicators:

- A pleasant smell, good taste, and fizziness after bottling are signs of successful fermentation.

Using dried fruit:

- Dried fruits like figs, dates, cranberries, and raisins supply essential nutrients to the grains. Use a higher quantity when substituting figs with other dried fruits.

Making kefir without figs:

- If not using figs, compensate with mineral-rich water or low-processed sugar to provide necessary minerals.

Lemon in kefir:

- Lemon or citrus slices can create an ideal acidic environment for fermentation.

Consumption recommendations:

- Start with one glass of kefir per day and increase gradually to allow your body to adjust.

Safety of water kefir:

- Water kefir is safe when prepared with clean equipment and proper ingredients.

Growing kefir grains:

- For healthy growth, maintain regular fermentation cycles, ensure consistent temperature (20–25°C), and provide balanced mineral content. Nutritional boosts like bicarbonate of soda, eggshell, or molasses can be beneficial.

Milk vs. Water Kefir Grains:

- Milk and water kefir grains are distinct; milk kefir grains should not be used in water kefir recipes.

Alternative Liquids for Water Kefir:

- Experimentation is possible with other liquids, but grains may weaken over time. Use extra grains for experiments.

Plant-based milk kefir:

- Coconut and soya milk are suitable for making plant-based milk kefir. Avoid using almond or oat milk as they may not support grain health.

Kefir grain composition:

- Kefir grains comprise a complex symbiotic matrix of bacteria and yeast, forming unique, crystal-shaped structures.

By adhering to these guidelines, you can ensure a rewarding kefir-making experience, whether you're a seasoned fermenter or new to the world of probiotic foods. Enjoy the delicious and healthful benefits of kefir in your diet.

	MILK KEFIR	WATER KEFIR
Starter	Milk kefir grains	Water kefir grains
Ingredients	Milk	Water, sugar & fruits
Fermentation time	24 to 48h	24 to 48h

104. RECIPE FOR MILK KEFIR

Making milk kefir is a straightforward and rewarding process that brings a host of probiotic benefits right into your kitchen. It requires just a bit of care and attention to ensure that the kefir grains are not neglected for prolonged periods. Following this guide, you can easily create your milk kefir, resulting in a delicious and tangy beverage that is as nutritious as it is versatile.

INGREDIENTS:

» 4 cups raw or whole milk cow, (sheep or goat milk)
» 4 tsp kefir grains

EQUIPMENT:

» Fermentation jar or container
» Spoon or ladle
» Non-metallic strainer

» Bowl
» Funnel
» Bottle or container for storing kefir

INSTRUCTIONS:

1. Prepare Grains: Start by acquiring kefir grains. You can find them through online stores or receive them as a gift from a fellow fermenter.
2. Clean the Jar: Ensure your fermentation jar is clean and dry to prevent any unwanted bacteria from affecting your kefir.
3. Combine Ingredients: Place the kefir grains in the jar. Add the milk and stir gently to mix everything.
4. Fermentation: Cover the jar loosely to allow gases to escape and let it sit at room temperature (68–78°F) for 24–48 hours. If you can, stir the mixture a couple of times during this period to help even fermentation.
5. Ready to enjoy: O Your kefir is ready when it has thickened to a consistency similar to drinkable yogurt and has a pleasant tanginess.
6. Strain and store: Use a non-metallic strainer to separate the kefir grains from the liquid. Bottle the strained kefir and refrigerate. The grains are ready to start a new batch immediately or can be stored for later use.

Tips for Success:

» Milk choice: You can use any milk like cow, sheep, or goat milk, but avoid using plant-based milk as they don't contain the lactose needed by the grains.
» Cheese making: For an extra treat, strain your kefir through a cheesecloth to make a soft cheese, using the leftover whey in other fermentation projects.
» Fermenting cream: Transform cream into delicious fermented butter by following the same process as with milk.

» Grain storage: If you're taking a break, grains can be stored in the fridge with a little milk for 1–2 weeks, frozen for up to 6 months, or dried for longer storage. Note that drying may have variable results.
» Sharing grains: As your grains multiply, consider sharing them with others in the kefir community.
» Avoid metal: Metal utensils can interfere with the fermentation process. Use them sparingly and opt for plastic, wood, or silicone when possible.

Remember, successful fermentation not only yields great food but also fosters a sense of community and sharing. Happy fermenting!

105. CHEESE FROM MILK KEFIR

Discover the simplicity of making your milk kefir cheese at home, without the need for specialized equipment or ingredients. This easy-to-follow recipe yields a delicious, creamy cheese perfect for various culinary uses.

EQUIPMENT NEEDED:

» Colander lined with cheesecloth or coffee filters
» Alternatively, a clean cotton bag

INGREDIENTS:

» 1 quart (about 1 liter) milk kefir
» ½ tsp salt (adjust according to taste)
» Optional: Spices and pepper to enhance flavor

INSTRUCTIONS:

1. Strain the kefir: Pour the milk kefir into the colander or cotton bag to separate the whey. The whey should drip off clear and transparent. This process can be done overnight in the refrigerator for convenience.
2. Press for firmness: For a firmer cheese texture, press down on the strained kefir. Place a weight, such as a heavy plate, on top and leave it in a cool place under pressure for a few hours.
3. Season the cheese: After achieving a cream cheese consistency, transfer the cheese to a bowl. Stir in the salt and any desired spices until evenly distributed.
4. Mold and chill: Transfer the cheese mixture into a serving dish or mold for shaping. Refrigerate for a few hours to set before serving.

Serving Suggestions:

» Serve this versatile cheese with crackers, on sandwiches, or as a dip.

» Elevate special occasions by pairing it with blinis or savory pancakes, complemented by smoked salmon or fresh herbs.

Safety Precautions:

» Ensure all utensils and containers are cleaned thoroughly with hot, soapy water.
» Sterilize cheesecloths or cotton bags by boiling them for ten minutes before use.

» Use boiled then cooled milk for recipes involving powdered starters.
» Discard any kefir or kefir cheese that exhibits unusual smells, tastes, or visible mold.

Storing Kefir Cheese:

» Freshly made kefir cheese can last in the refrigerator for up to one week, provided it retains its fresh, tangy aroma and shows no signs of mold.
» While aging kefir cheese is possible, it requires careful attention to hygiene and storage conditions to avoid spoilage.

106. TZATZIKI MADE WITH KEFIR

Dive into the refreshing world of homemade tzatziki with this kefir cheese-based recipe. This sauce brings a creamy, tangy twist to traditional tzatziki, making it a perfect complement to a wide array of dishes.

INGREDIENTS:

» 1 cup kefir cheese
» ½ cup grated cucumber
» ¼ cup fresh mint
» 1 garlic clove, (or 1 tbsp chopped garlic scape)
» ½ lemon juiced
» Salt and pepper, to taste
» 1 tsp olive oil

INSTRUCTIONS:

1. Prepare ingredients: Start by finely chopping the mint and crushing the garlic. If using garlic scapes, chop them finely for a milder garlic flavor.
2. Mix: In a medium-sized mixing bowl, combine the kefir cheese with the chopped mint, garlic, or garlic scape, and grated cucumber. Stir well. Add the lemon juice to the mixture and stir again until all ingredients are well incorporated. If the sauce seems too thick, you can adjust its consistency by adding a little more grated cucumber.
3. Season: Taste the mixture and season with salt and pepper according to your preference. Mix well to ensure the seasoning is evenly distributed throughout the sauce.
4. Chill: Cover the bowl and refrigerate the tzatziki sauce for at least an hour to allow the flavors to meld together and the sauce to chill thoroughly.
5. Serve: Just before serving, give the tzatziki one final stir, check for seasoning adjustments, and transfer to a serving bowl. Drizzle olive oil over the top for an added layer of flavor.

Storage and Serving Suggestions:

6. Storage: This kefir cheese tzatziki sauce can be stored in an airtight container in the refrigerator for up to 1 week.
7. Serving: Serve the tzatziki sauce with warm pita bread as a delightful dip, as a refreshing spread on sandwiches, or alongside grilled meats and vegetables for a cooling complement to your meal.

This kefir cheese tzatziki sauce recipe marries the probiotic benefits of kefir with the crisp flavors of cucumber and mint, creating a versatile sauce that's as nutritious as it is delicious. Whether you're dressing up for a weekday dinner or entertaining guests, this tzatziki is sure to be a hit.

107. MASCARPONE CHEESE WITH KEFIR

Elevate the everyday to the exceptional with this straightforward and delightful homemade mascarpone cheese recipe, utilizing milk kefir grains. This technique allows you to recreate the luxurious, creamy texture of traditional Italian mascarpone in your kitchen, all with minimal effort and outstanding flavor.

EQUIPMENT NEEDED:

» Glass container
» Colander with large holes
» Cloth and rubber band for covering

INGREDIENTS:

» 2 cups (500 ml) 35% cream
» 1 tbsp active milk kefir grains

INSTRUCTIONS:

1. Mix cream and kefir grains: In the glass container, thoroughly combine the cream with the active milk kefir grains. Ensure the grains are evenly dispersed throughout the cream.
2. Fermentation: Cover the container with a cloth, securing it in place with a rubber band. This setup allows the mixture to breathe while fermenting. Leave it at room temperature (ideally between 68°F to 72°F) for 24 hours.
3. Strain the mixture: After fermentation, use the colander to strain the mixture, separating the kefir grains from the now-thickened cream. Reserve the grains for future use or start another batch of mascarpone immediately.
4. Thicken the Mascarpone: To achieve the classic mascarpone texture, transfer the cream to a fine muslin cloth. Hang it over a bowl to drain any excess whey for about 12 hours, or until it reaches your desired thickness.
5. Refrigeration: Once thickened to your liking, transfer the mascarpone into a clean glass container for storage. Keep it refrigerated.

Serving and Storage:

» Versatile Use: Your homemade mascarpone can be used in various recipes, just like any store-bought version. It's perfect for desserts like tiramisu, as a spread on toast, or as a luxurious addition to pasta sauces.

» Storage: Keep the mascarpone refrigerated, where it will stay fresh for up to one month. Ensure the container is sealed properly to maintain its freshness and prevent it from absorbing other flavors from the fridge.

This kefir mascarpone cheese recipe presents an enjoyable way to incorporate a sophisticated ingredient into your cooking, enhanced with the probiotic advantages of kefir grains. Perfect for creating classic Italian desserts, adding richness to sauces, enjoying as a spread on freshly toasted bread, or adding a creamy touch to pizzas, this mascarpone promises to elevate your culinary creations.

108. MAKING BUTTER AT HOME

Create your cultured butter from whipping cream with this simple and enjoyable recipe. This process yields a rich, tangy butter that can be savored in its classic, salted form or enhanced with your choice of herbs and spices. Transform whipping cream into home-made butter, offering versatility in flavor for a unique and delightful taste experience.

INGREDIENTS:

» 2 cups whipping cream (heavy cream)
» 2 tbsp culture (options include milk kefir grains, cultured sour cream, or cultured buttermilk; alternatively, use unpasteurized cream for natural fermentation)
» A pinch salt (less than ¼ tsp), adjusted to taste

INSTRUCTIONS:

1. Ferment the cream: In a large jar, mix the whipping cream with your choice of culture. Let it sit at room temperature for at least 12 hours to allow fermentation. This step introduces a depth of flavor and aids in the separation process.
2. Whip the cream: After fermentation, use a hand mixer, food processor, stand mixer, or even shake the jar vigorously to whip the cream. Continue until the cream thickens and eventually separates into butterfat and buttermilk. This process typically takes about 10 minutes.
3. Separate the butter: Once the mixture has separated, use a spoon to gather the butterfat and transfer it to a bowl. Press firmly to expel as much buttermilk as possible, retaining the buttermilk for other uses.
4. Rinse the butter: Rinse the collected butter under cold water while pressing to remove the remaining buttermilk. Repeat this rinsing and pressing process until the water runs clear, ensuring all buttermilk is extracted to increase the butter's shelf life.
5. Flavor the butter: After draining, add a pinch of salt to the butter. At this stage, feel free to incorporate additional flavors such as herbs, garlic, or spices according to your preferences.
6. Store: Transfer your finished butter into a container. If unsalted, refrigerate it; salted butter can be stored at room temperature for up to a week.

Notes:

» This method is suitable for making butter in a 1-quart mason jar, yielding about 1 cup of butter and 1 cup of buttermilk.

» The resulting buttermilk is perfect for baking or as a refreshing drink. However, it might be thinner and sweeter than commercial buttermilk, which could affect some recipes.

Homemade cultured butter offers a superior taste and texture compared to store-bought varieties. Whether spread on freshly baked bread, used in cooking or as a base for compound butter, this cultured butter is sure to elevate your dishes with its rich, nuanced flavor. Enjoy the satisfaction of creating this dairy delight in your kitchen!

109. RECIPE FOR WATER KEFIR

Water kefir is a fermented, slightly effervescent drink that's not only delicious but also packed with probiotics. Making your own at home is straightforward and offers a healthier alternative to commercial soft drinks. Here's how to get started:

TOOLS NEEDED:

» Fermentation-friendly glass jar
» Wooden stirring utensil
» Cloth, cheesecloth, or kitchen towel for covering
» Rubber band to secure the cover
» Fine mesh strainer

INGREDIENTS:

» Water kefir grains (tibicos)
» 5–10% sugar per liter of water (e.g., 50–100g sugar for each liter)
» Fresh lemon juice
» Optional: Dried fruit (raisins, dates, etc.)
» Chlorine-free water

INSTRUCTIONS:

1. Prepare sugar water: In the glass jar, dissolve ¼ cup to ½ cup of sugar in 4 cups (950ml) of chlorine-free water. Stir well to ensure the sugar is fully dissolved.
2. Acidify: Add the juice of half a lemon per liter of water to create a slightly acidic environment that discourages mold growth.
3. Add extras: Optionally, enrich the water with dried fruits for additional nutrients and flavor.
4. Introduce kefir grains: Place the water kefir grains into the jar.
5. Cover and ferment: Cover the jar with a cloth and secure it with a rubber band. This setup allows the drink to breathe while preventing contaminants from getting in. Let it ferment at room temperature (20–24°C) for 24–48 hours.
6. Prepare for next batch: After fermentation, prepare a new batch of sugar water (repeat steps 1–5).
7. Strain: Use the strainer to separate the grains from the finished kefir water.
8. Restart fermentation: Transfer the grains to the new batch of sugar water for another round of fermentation.
9. Savor: The water kefir is now ready to be flavored, bottled, or refrigerated for consumption.

Storing Water Kefir Grains:

» Pause fermentation: If you need to take a break, the grains can be refrigerated, dried, or frozen after being active for 3–4 weeks. However, the results of reviving dormant grains can be unpredictable.

» Community sharing: Instead of dormancy, consider sharing active grains with friends and family. This approach not only preserves the vitality of the grains but also fosters a sense of community and keeps the tradition of fermenting alive.

Water kefir is a versatile drink that can be customized with various flavors and fruits, making it a delightful addition to your daily routine. Enjoy the process of crafting this probiotic-rich beverage and explore different variations to find your favorite combinations.

110. COCONUT WATER KEFIR MADE AT HOME

Discover the world of fermented beverages with this easy-to-make and refreshing coconut water kefir drink. It's not only delicious and refreshing but also packed with electrolytes, beneficial for the immune system, and advantageous for gut health, contributing to a well-balanced digestive system. The beneficial bacteria present in kefir also play a vital role in strengthening the immune system, enhancing the body's natural defenses.

Incorporating just half a cup of this drink with your meals can provide a revitalizing boost to digestion and enhance overall well-being

INGREDIENTS:

» ¼ cup kefir grains or a water kefir starter
» 5 cups coconut water
» ½ cup your preferred juice (lemon, lime, cherry, tangerine, etc.)

INSTRUCTIONS:

1. **Initial Fermentation:**

» In a large jar, combine the kefir grains or starter with the coconut water.
» Cover the jar with cheesecloth and secure it with a rubber band. This setup allows the mixture to breathe while keeping out any contaminants.
» Allow the mixture to ferment at room temperature for up to 48 hours. Note that warmer conditions may speed up the fermentation process.
» Once fermentation is complete, strain the kefir to remove the grains. Preserve these grains for your next batch.

2. **Second Fermentation for Fizziness:**

» After straining, blend the kefir with your choice of juice. This step introduces additional flavors and sugars for the kefir to ferment further.
» Pour this mixture into a sealable bottle, leaving some space at the top for the gases that will be produced.
» Let the bottle ferment at room temperature for up to 48 hours, or until you notice it has become fizzy. Be sure to check the pressure occasionally to avoid over-carbonation.
» Refrigerate the coconut water kefir to slow fermentation and chill before enjoying.

Tips:

» Variety: Experiment with different juice flavors to find your preferred taste.
» Storage: Always keep a batch of kefir fermenting so you have a continuous supply.
» Health benefits: Regularly consuming coconut water kefir can lead to improved hydration, better digestion, and a strengthened immune system.

Enjoy crafting this probiotic-rich, effervescent drink and reap the numerous health benefits it offers!

Kombucha

Kombucha: The Ancient Health Elixir

Kombucha, a fermented black tea known for its distinctive tangy taste, has been celebrated for its health benefits for centuries. Originating from East Asia around 2,000 years ago, kombucha is created through the fermentation of tea using a symbiotic culture of bacteria and yeast (SCOBY). This process not only imparts a unique flavor but also enriches the beverage with probiotics, beneficial acids, and vitamins, contributing to its reputation as a health elixir.

Health Benefits of Kombucha

- **Gut health:** The probiotics produced during the fermentation process support a healthy gut microbiota, which is crucial for digestion and nutrient absorption.
- **Immune system boost:** Probiotics in kombucha help strengthen the immune system by enhancing gut barrier function and supporting the growth of beneficial gut bacteria.
- **Heart health:** Some studies suggest that kombucha can improve cholesterol levels, contributing to better heart health.
- **Brain health:** The antioxidants in kombucha may offer protective effects for brain cells and improve mental function.

Nutritional Profile of Kombucha (Per Half-Quart Bottle)

- Calories: 60
- Carbohydrates: 14 grams
- Sugar: 4 grams
- Sodium: 20 milligrams
- Vitamin B2: 0.34 grams
- Vitamin B6: 0.4 milligrams
- Vitamin B1: 0.3 milligrams
- Vitamin B3: 4 milligrams
- Vitamin B12: 1.2 micrograms

Note: The nutritional content can vary significantly between different brands and homemade versions, particularly in terms of sugar content and the concentration of probiotics and vitamins.

Making Kombucha at Home

Creating kombucha involves brewing sweetened tea, adding a SCOBY, and allowing it to ferment in a clean, glass container at room temperature for 7 to 14 days. After the initial fermentation, the kombucha can be flavored with fruits, herbs, or spices during a second fermentation phase to enhance its taste

Safety Tips

- Ensure all equipment is thoroughly cleaned to prevent contamination.
- During fermentation, kombucha should be stored away from direct sunlight in a well-ventilated area.
- Be mindful of the potential for excess carbonation; bottles should be burped regularly to release pressure.
- Those with a compromised immune system or pregnant women should consult a healthcare provider before regularly consuming kombucha.

Kombucha's blend of sweet and tart flavors, combined with its health-promoting properties, makes it a fascinating beverage to explore. Whether purchased commercially or brewed at home, kombucha offers a delicious way to support overall health and wellness.

111. KOMBUCHA BREWED AT HOME

Embrace the art of kombucha brewing with this straightforward recipe. Kombucha, a fermented tea drink, is cherished for its tangy flavor and myriad health benefits. Follow these simple steps to create your kombucha at home.

EQUIPMENT NEEDED:

» Food-grade jar or container with a tap (optional)
» Towel or paper towel
» Rubber band to secure the cover

INGREDIENTS:

» 4 cups non-chlorinated water
» 2 tbsp black tea (English Breakfast or Assam Tea are excellent choices)
» ½ cup sugar
» 2/5 cup (100 ml) mature kombucha (from a previous batch or store-bought)
» 1 SCOBY (Symbiotic Culture of Bacteria and Yeast)

INSTRUCTIONS:

1. Brew the tea: Heat the water to the appropriate temperature for your chosen tea. Steep the tea for 5–7 minutes, ensuring not to over-steep to avoid bitterness.
2. Sweeten the tea: Remove the tea leaves and dissolve the sugar in the hot tea. This will be the food for your SCOBY.
3. Cool the tea: Allow the sweetened tea to cool to room temperature to avoid damaging the SCOBY.
4. Combine ingredients: In your container, combine the cooled sweet tea, mature kombucha, and SCOBY. The mature kombucha helps acidify the environment, providing a safe start for fermentation.
5. Cover and ferment: Secure a towel or paper towel over the opening of the container with a rubber band. This setup lets the kombucha breathe while keeping out contaminants.
6. Fermentation period: Let the kombucha ferment at room temperature, ideally between 70° to 85°F (21° to 29°C), for 7–21 days. The fermentation time will depend on your taste preference; a longer fermentation results in a tarter kombucha.
7. Harvest and repeat: Once the kombucha reaches your desired level of acidity, reserve a portion of the liquid to use as a starter for your next batch. Refrigerate the rest for drinking or proceed to a second fermentation for added flavor.
8. SCOBY care: With each batch, you'll grow a new "mother" SCOBY. Keep extra SCOBYs in a "SCOBY hotel"—a container filled with mature kombucha to keep them healthy.

Tips for Success:

» The flavor of kombucha can vary greatly depending on fermentation time. Experiment to find your perfect balance.

» Starting with a small daily amount is advised if you're new to drinking kombucha.

» The position of the SCOBY in the container is not critical; it may float, sink, or even develop sideways.

» In case of mold, discard the entire batch and start over with a new SCOBY and mature kombucha to ensure safety.

» Overly acidic kombucha can be repurposed as a vinegar substitute in recipes or undergo a second fermentation with added flavors to increase carbonation.

Savoring Your Kombucha:

Customize your kombucha by experimenting with secondary fermentations. Add fruits, herbs, or spices to the bottled kombucha and let it ferment for an additional 2–3 days to infuse the flavors and enhance fizziness.

Creating kombucha at home allows you to personalize your brew and enjoy the probiotic benefits of this ancient beverage. Whether enjoyed plain or flavored, kombucha is a delightful addition to a healthy lifestyle.

112. KOMBUCHA WITH ELDERBERRY AND GINGER

Elevate your kombucha brewing experience with this Elderberry-Ginger Kombucha Elixir, a perfect blend of health-boosting ingredients. Elderberries, renowned for their immune-supporting properties, and ginger, known for its digestive benefits, come together in this delicious tonic. This recipe starts with crafting an elderberry syrup, which is then infused into already prepared kombucha, creating a fizzy, flavorful, and healthful drink.

INGREDIENTS:

- » 3 quarts prepared kombucha tea
- » 4 ½ tbsp dried elderberries
- » ¾ cup coconut palm sugar
- » 1 ½ cups water
- » 3 tbsp fresh ginger, chopped

INSTRUCTIONS:

1. **Make the elderberryisyrup:**
» In a saucepan, combine the elderberries and chopped ginger with water. Bring the mixture to a boil, then simmer on medium heat until the liquid is reduced to about half a cup, approximately 15–20 minutes.
» Remove the saucepan from the heat and stir in the coconut palm sugar until it's completely dissolved.
» Strain the syrup through a fine-mesh sieve into a jar, discarding the solids. Allow the syrup to cool to room temperature.

2. **Combine with kombucha:**
» Pour the cooled elderberry syrup into a large jar containing the prepared kombucha tea. Stir thoroughly to combine.
» Carefully transfer the kombucha mixture into flip-top bottles, leaving some space to avoid excessive pressure build-up.

3. **Second fermentation:**
» Allow the bottles to ferment at room temperature for 2–3 days to achieve the desired level of fizziness.
» The kombucha can be enjoyed immediately after this period or stored in the refrigerator for up to 6 months to maintain its freshness.

Notes:

» Starter culture swap: For a different twist, you can use water kefir or a ginger bug in place of kombucha to create an elderberry soda or elderberry kefir.

» Herb mix-ins: Enhance the flavor profile by adding other beneficial herbs like hibiscus, rosehips, orange peel, cloves, or cinnamon chips during the syrup-making process.

» Sugar alternatives: Feel free to experiment with different sweeteners such as maple sugar, organic white sugar, or honey, adjusting to taste and dietary preferences.

Tips:

» Safety first: Ensure your bottles are clean and capable of handling pressure to prevent any fermentation accidents.

» Serving suggestion: Serve chilled for a refreshing and invigorating tonic.

» Health benefits: This kombucha elixir not only tastes great but also offers a natural way to support your immune system, making it a perfect beverage for any season.

Delight in crafting this elderberry-ginger kombucha elixir, a beverage that promises both delightful flavors and numerous health benefits. Whether you're a seasoned kombucha brewer or a newcomer to the world of fermented drinks, this recipe is sure to become a favorite.

CHAPTER 12
FAQS AND PROBLEM SOLVING

This section serves as a quick reference guide, answering frequently posed questions and offering insights along with solutions to enhance your preservation techniques. Alongside the questions, you will discover an extensive Troubleshooting Guide that delves into common problems, their causes, and solutions within the realms of pickling and fermentation.

We meticulously examine the prevalent issues encountered in these processes, offering a detailed analysis of the reasons behind these complications and proposing effective solutions. Each issue is identified alongside its root cause, followed by practical, straightforward remedies. This guide is designed to provide you with the necessary knowledge and tools to master the intricacies of pickling and fermenting, ensuring the success of your culinary endeavors.

FAQ

1. **Is Fake Salt Suitable for Brine Preparation?**
   Utilizing flake salt for brine is not advisable due to its inconsistent density. Opting for granulated or pickling salt is preferable.
2. **Can I Reuse Brine from Quick-Process Pickles?**
   The pickling solution can be reused if it's fresh and hasn't been used before, by storing it in the refrigerator for later use. However, if it has already been used, it's safe to reuse within 1–2 days for dressings or marinades, provided there's no mold present.
3. **What Makes the Brine in Dill Pickles Turn Pink?**
   Pink discoloration in the pickle brine may occur if the dill used is too mature or if there's yeast contamination. Discarding the pickles is advisable if yeast contamination is observed.
4. **How Can I Substitute Dill in Pickling Recipes?**
   You can substitute the specified type of dill with either three heads of fresh dill or 1–2 tbsp of dill seeds for each quart of pickles.
5. **Are Burpless Cucumbers Good for Pickling?**
   While Burpless cucumbers are not suitable for fermented pickles, they can be used for fresh pickling, especially if they are small in size.
6. **Why Should I Add Grape Leaves to Pickle Jars?**
   Adding a grape leaf helps suppress enzymes that could otherwise soften the pickles. This measure can be skipped by simply cutting off the blossom ends of the cucumbers.
7. **Why Did My Garlic Turn Green or Blue in the Pickles?**
   The color change in garlic to green or blue can result from interaction with metals or due to natural pigments in garlic, but it doesn't affect the safety of the pickles for consumption.
8. **Is It Safe to Use Aluminum Pans for Pickling?**
   Consuming pickles from a batch that has been scalded in an aluminum pan is generally safe, though it's recommended to avoid using aluminum when working with lime in future preparations.
9. **Can Diabetics Use Artificial Sweeteners in Sweet Pickles?**

Direct substitution of sugar with artificial sweeteners in pickle recipes is not recommended. A better approach is to rinse dill pickle slices and then add artificial sweetener to achieve a similar taste profile.

Problems and Solutions

Comprehensive Troubleshooting Guide
Problems, Causes, and Solutions in Pickling and Fermenting

PROBLEM	REASON	SOLUTION
Soft and slimy pickles (don't eat if they seem spoiled).	1. Weak vinegar.	1. Utilize vinegar with a minimum of 5% acidity.
	2. Not enough brine.	2. Ensure cucumbers are fully covered in brine.
	3. Incorrect pickle processing to eliminate germs.	3. Process pickles in a canner after filling jars.
	4. Moldy garlic or spices.	4. Always select fresh spices.
	5. Failure or remove the blossom ends of cucumbers.	5. Cut off and discard at least 1/16th inch from the blossom end of the cucumbers.
Intense bitter flavor	1. Overcooking spices in vinegar or using excessive amounts.	1. Adhere to the recipe's guidelines for spice quantities and boiling duration.
	2. Vinegar too strong.	2. Employ vinegar with the correct strength (5% acidity).
	3. Arid climate conditions.	3. No specific prevention, the bitter taste often originates from the skin or peel of fruits and vegetables.
	4. Using salt alternative.	4. Be aware that potassium chloride, commonly found in these substitutes, can lead to bitterness.
Shriveled pickles	1. Too concentrated brine, syrup, or vinegar.	1. Adhere to a trusted recipe, using the specified amounts of salt, sugar, and 5% acidity vinegar.
	2. Overcooking or excessive processing.	2. Process as per the recipe instructions.
	3. Effects of dry weather.	3. No solution for dry weather as it naturally affects the texture.

PROBLEM	REASON	SOLUTION
Dark or discolored pickles (do not consume if made with brass, copper or zinc equipment)	1. Using hard water with high mineral content.	1. Use soft water.
	2. Employing ground spices.	2. Use whole spices instead.
	3. Leaving spices in the pickle jars.	3. Place spices in a cheesecloth bag for easy removal.
	4. Utilizing brass, iron, copper, or zinc utensils.	4. Use enamelware, glass, stainless steel, or stoneware utensils safe for food.
	5. Using Iodized salt.	5. Choose canning or pickling salt.
Spotted, dull, or faded pickle color	1. Overexposure to light.	1. Store jars in a dark, cool, dry place.
	2. Using low-quality Cucumbers.	2. Select high-quality produce, considering factors like weather and soil conditions.
White sediment in a jar.	1. Salt with an anti-caking agent or additives.	1. Use specific canning or pickling salt.

Troubleshooting Fermented Pickles

PROBLEM	REASON	SOLUTION
Soft or slippery pickles (do not consume if they appear spoiled).	1. Weak salt brine during fermentation.	1. Adhere to the salt concentration recommended in the recipe.
	2. Fermenting cucumbers at excessively high temperatures.	2. Ferment cucumbers at an ideal temperature range of 70° and 75°F.
	3. Not enough brine.	3. Ensure cucumbers are fully submerged in brine.
	4. Inadequate processing for microorganisms' destruction.	4. Process pickles in a canner after filling jars.
	5. Use of stale garlic or spices.	5. Use fresh spices.
	6. Blossom ends not removed from cucumbers.	6. Cut off and discard at least 1/16th inch from the blossom end of cucumbers.

PROBLEM	REASON	SOLUTION
Strong, bitter taste	1. Overcooking spices in vinegar or using too much.	1. Follow precise spice amounts and boiling time as per the recipe.
	2. Using overly strong vinegar.	2. Use vinegar with (5% acidity).
	3. Natural bitterness due to dry weather conditions.	3. Understand that some bitterness is natural and unavoidable.
	4. Bitterness from salt substitutes containing potassium chloride.	4. Be aware of the bitter taste caused by potassium chloride in salt substitutes.
Hollow pickles	1. Using cucumbers that are too large for brining.	1. Use smaller-sized cucumbers suitable for brining.
	2. Incorrect fermentation process.	2. Ensure the brine is of the right concentration and cover the product entirely. Continue the curing process until fermentation is fully complete.
	3. Delay in starting the brining process after harvesting cucumbers.	3. Begin the fermentation within 24 hours of harvesting the cucumbers.
	4. Inherent growth issues in cucumbers.	4. There's no prevention for growth defects. Hollow cucumbers often float during washing; these should be set aside for use in relishes rather than fermented pickles.

PROBLEM	REASON	SOLUTION
Shriveled pickles	1. Using overly strong brine, syrup, or vinegar.	1. Stick to a trusted recipe for correct salt, sugar, and 5% acidity vinegar ratios.
	2. Delay in brining after cucumber harvest.	2. Start the brining process within 24 hours of harvesting.
	3. Excessive cooking or processing.	3. Precisely follow the recipe's cooking and processing instructions.
	4. Effect of dry weather.	4. Accept that dry weather can impact pickle quality and taste.
Scum formation on brine surface during cucumber curing.	1. Accumulation of wild yeasts and bacteria.	1. Regularly remove the scum as it forms.
Dark or discolored pickles (avoid if made with certain metals).	1. Use of hard water with high mineral content.	1. Use soft water.
	2. Utilizing ground spices.	2. Choose whole spices over ground ones.
	3. Leaving spices in pickle jars.	3. Put spices in a cheesecloth bag for easy removal before canning.
	4. Using specific metal utensils (brass, iron, copper, or zinc).	4. Use safe food-grade materials like enamelware, glass, stainless steel, or stoneware.
	5. Employing Iodized salt in the process.	5. Use canning or pickling salt instead of iodized varieties.

PROBLEM	REASON	SOLUTION
Spotted, dull, or faded pickle color	1. Inadequate curing (brining) of cucumbers.	1. Ensure the use of properly concentrated brine and complete the fermentation process.
	2. Overexposure to light.	2. Store jars in a place that is cool, dark, and dry.
	3. Using low-quality cucumbers.	3. Select high-quality, cucumbers, grown in favorable conditions.
White sediment in a jar.	1. Bacteria activity during fermentation.	1. This is a natural occurrence; no specific prevention.
	2. Presence of anti-caking agents or additives in salt.	2. Use canning or pickling salt that doesn't contain additives.

CONCLUSION

As we conclude our exploration into the enriching world of pickling and fermenting, I hope you feel equipped and inspired to embrace these time-honored traditions in your kitchen. From uncovering the history and significance of food preservation methods to enhancing your gut health with fermented foods, we have navigated through the fundamentals and beyond, unlocking the secrets of selection, preparation, and safe storage.

Reflecting on our journey, it becomes evident that preserving food transcends simply extending the shelf life of our harvests. It's about rekindling a connection to the land, to our heritage, and to the essence of nourishment itself. The virtues of fermented foods go well beyond their taste, offering wellness and vitality with every bite. As you have learned to initiate your fermentation projects, to discern when your foods are perfectly fermented, and to address any arising issues, remember that each step is an enriching learning experience, deepening your relationship with food and the natural world.

Whether you have already ventured to try some of the recipes shared or are poised to start, recognize that the journey of food preservation is one of discovery, creativity, and fulfillment. The FAQ and problem-solving sections will continue to support you as you delve further into experimentation and enhance your practice.

As you turn the final page of this book, consider it not as the conclusion of your exploration but as the beginning of further culinary endeavors. The realm of pickling and fermenting is broad and diverse, offering endless possibilities limited only by your imagination. Continue to explore, to experiment, and most importantly, to enjoy the journey. The flavors you will discover, the health benefits you will reap, and the sense of accomplishment you will experience are merely the starting point.

Thank you for being with me on this journey of preparation. May your kitchen always be filled with the lively aromas of fermentation and the vivid hues of pickles—a constant testament to the generosity and beauty of nature. Cheers to many more adventures in pickling and fermenting!

Thank You for Reading My Book

I hope you found the information useful and stimulating. As a special thank you, here is an exclusive bonus for you: the **"Food Preserving Planner."** This planner will help you organize and record all your food preservation activities.

★ YOUR BONUS! ★
"FOOD PRESERVING PLANNER"

The planner includes:

1. Planning and Scheduling: Plan your activities, key dates, seasonal products, and milestones with the Annual Calendar. The Activity List guides you through daily and monthly tasks for organized management.

2. Recipes and Preparations: Save your favorite recipes and necessary details in your Recipe Space for safe and precise preparation.

3. Preservation Logs: Track all activities in the General Log for accurate management of the preservation process.

4. Monitoring and Evaluation: Assess the quality of preserved foods, monitor fermentation times and pH levels, and record observations and adjustments to continuously improve the process.

5. Management and Inventory: Keep track of supplies with the Preservation Inventory, note improvements, and use the Jar Labels for easy identification of contents.

SCAN HERE TO DOWNLOADED IT!

Share Your Feedback!

Dear Reader,

Thank you for reading "Pickling and Fermenting Cookbook for Preppers." I hope you enjoyed the content as much as I enjoyed writing it.

Your feedback is important to me. An honest review on Amazon helps other readers discover my work and support my growth as an author.

If you enjoyed the book, please take a few minutes to leave a review on Amazon. Even a brief review can make a significant difference!

SCAN HERE TO LEAVE YOUR REVIEW!

If you have any questions, please feel free to reach out to me directly at: info@sophiemagnant.com

Thank you for your support!

Best regards,
Sophie Magnant

ALPHABETICAL RECIPE INDEX

A

Apple Chutney with Sweet and Spicy Flavors — 80
Apple Tomato Chutney — 78
Asparagus Pickles — 50
Avocado Pickles — 75

B

Banana Pepper Rings Pickles — 46
Beet-Infused Sauerkraut — 110
Beetroot and Ginger Sauerkraut — 110
Beetroot Pickles — 45
Berry Pickle with a Sweet and Sour Taste — 73
Bittersweet Spiced Plum Pickles — 71
Bread and Butter Zucchini Pickles — 48
Brussels Sprouts Pickles with Turmeric — 51

C

Canned Chili Con Carne — 95
Canned Fish Recipe: Trout, Salmon, Bluefish — 97
Canned Meatballs in Salsa — 94
Canned Tuna Recipe — 99
Canning Recipe for Poultry; Chicken, Turkey, and More — 93
Carrot and Sauerkraut Mix — 111
Carrot Pickles — 46
Cauliflower Pickles with Turmeric and Ginger — 52
Cheese from Milk Kefir — 149
Cherries Pickled with Spices — 73
Cherry Tomatoes Fermented — 118
Cinnamon Fig Pickles — 64
Cinnamon Spiced Crabapples — 65
Classic Bread and Butter Pickles — 56
Classic Cabbage Sauerkraut — 108
Classic Shrimp Canning — 100
Classic Sourdough Bread — 141
Coconut Water Kefir Made at Home — 154
Cranberry Orange Chutney with a Tang — 79
Cranberry Relish Fermented — 133
Cucumber and Onions Refreshing Pickles — 60

D

Dilled Okra Pickles — 47
Dilled Pickled Beans — 44

E

Easy Kimchi Recipe — 125
Eggs Pickled with Dill — 88

F

Fennel and Orange Pickles — 62
Fermented Dill Cucumber Pickles — 113
Fermented Mixed Berries — 121
Fermented Radish Recipe — 115
Fermented Tangy Coleslaw — 112
Fig and Apple Balsamic Chutney — 83

G

Garlic Fermented in Honey — 116
Gingered Carrot Lacto-Fermented — 114
Ginger Spiced Crabapples — 63
Gluten-Free Sourdough Bread — 144
Green Tomato Dill Pickles — 44

H

Homemade Sauerkraut Made Easy — 110
Honey Fermented Plums — 122
Honey-Spiced Oranges — 69
Horseradish Pickles Sauce — 49
Hot Peppers Pickles — 50
Hot Sauce Lacto-Fermented — 135

J

Jalapeño Pineapple Relish — 86
Japanese Style Pickled Red Cabbage — 61

K

Ketchup Fermented at Home 137
Kimchi with Daikon Radish 126
Kiwi and Peach Chutney with Spices 82
Kombucha Brewed at Home 157
Kombucha with Elderberry and Ginger 159
Korean Cucumber Kimchi 126

L

Lacto-Fermented Turnips and Beets 114
Lemon Lacto-Fermented 117
Low Sodium Dill Pickle Slices 57
Low-sodium Sweet Pickle Slices 58

M

Making Butter at Home 152
Making Tempeh at Home 130
Marinated Mushrooms 47
Mascarpone Cheese with Kefir 151
Miso Made at Home 128
Mixed Peppers Relish 87

O

Onion Lacto-Fermented 115

P

Pear Chutney 81
Pear Pickles 66
Pickled Cantaloupe with a Sweet and Tangy Flavor 68
Pickled Eggs with Red Beet 90
Pickled Ginger, Japanese Style 72
Pickled Mustard Cucumber 55
Pickled Plums with Red Onions 70
Pickled Red Onion and Lime 62
Pineapple and Spicy Pickled Eggs 89
Plums Lacto-Fermented 120
Pumpkin and Cranberry Chutney with Spices 84

Q

Quick Dill Pickles 55
Quick Grapes Pickles 75
Quick Sweet Pickled Cucumbers 57
Quick Sweet Radish Pickles 59

R

Recipe for Canning Meat; Beef, Pork, and More 92
Recipe for Milk Kefir 148
Recipe for Starting Sourdough 139
Recipe for Water Kefir 153
Red Cabbage and Mango Fermentation 119
Rhubarb and Orange Chutney with a Tang 85
Rhubarb Pickles 74

S

Sauerkraut with Apple 111
Sauerkraut with Orange Flavor 111
Spicy Mustard Fermented 132
Starter for Gluten-Free Sourdough 143
Strawberry Jam with Lavender and Honey 74
Sugar-Free Sweet Pickle Slices 58
Sweet and Tangy Watermelon Rind Pickles 67
Sweet Green Cherry Tomato Pickles 54
Sweet Peppers Pickles 53
Sweet Pickled Watermelon Rind 66

T

Tangy Peach Pickles 69
Tomato and Jalapeño Fermented Salsa 134
Traditional Korean Baechu Kimchi 124
Traditional Oyster Canning 98
Turmeric-Ginger Pineapple Sauerkraut 112
Tzatziki Made with Kefir 150

W

Worcestershire Sauce Made at Home 136

CONVERSION CHART

 Conversion Chart

FOR THE KITCHEN

VOLUME MEASUREMENT CONVERSIONS

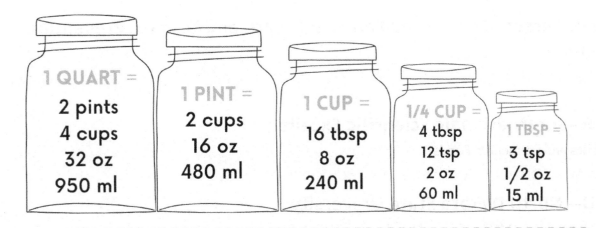

1 QUART =
2 pints
4 cups
32 oz
950 ml

1 PINT =
2 cups
16 oz
480 ml

1 CUP =
16 tbsp
8 oz
240 ml

1/4 CUP =
4 tbsp
12 tsp
2 oz
60 ml

1 TBSP =
3 tsp
1/2 oz
15 ml

CUPS	TABLESPOON	TEASPOON	MILLILITER
		1 tsp	5 ml
1/16 cup	1 tbsp	3 tsp	15 ml
1/8 cup	2 tbsp	6 tsp	30 ml
1/4 cup	4 tbsp	12 tsp	60 ml
1/3 cup	5 1/3 tbsp	16 tsp	80 ml
1/2 cup	8 tbsp	24 tsp	120 ml
2/3 cup	10 2/3 tbsp	32 tsp	160 ml
3/4 cup	12 tbsp	36 tsp	180 ml
1 cup	16 tbsp	48 tsp	240 ml

COOKING TEMPERATURE CONVERSIONS

CELCIUS	$F = (C \times 1.8) + 32$
FAHRENHEIT	$C = (F - 32) \times .5556$

RESOURCES

NCHFP—National Center for Home Food Preservation:

https://nchfp.uga.edu/#gsc.tab=0

CDC—Center for Disease Control and Prevention:

Food Safety Home—Canning and Botulism

https://www.cdc.gov/foodsafety/communication/home-canning-and-botulism.html

Science Direct—Fermented Foods in Health and Disease Prevention:

Book 2016

https://www.sciencedirect.com/book/9780128023099/fermented-foods-in-health-and-disease-prevention

ISAPP—Internationale Scientific Excellence:

Probiotics and Fermented Foods

https://isappscience.org/for-scientists/resources/fermented-foods/

NDSU—North Dakota State University:

Food Preservation: Making Pickled Products (2019)

https://www.ndsu.edu/agriculture/extension/publications/food-preservation-making-pickled-products

11479838R00096